Myths of Leadership

D1382436

Business Myths Series

Myths of Branding Simon Bailey and Andy Milligan
Myths of Leadership Jo Owen
Myths of Management Stefan Stern and Cary Cooper
Myths of Social Media Michelle Carvill and Ian MacRae
Myths of Strategy Jérôme Barthélemy
Myths of Work Ian MacRae

The above titles are available from all good bookshops.

For further information on these and other Kogan Page titles, or to order online, visit the Kogan Page website at: www.koganpage.com.

Jo Owen

MYTHS OF
LEADERSHIP

Dispel the misconceptions and
become an inspirational leader

2ND EDITION

KoganPage

First published in Great Britain and the United States in 2019 by Kogan Page Limited
Second edition 2023

2nd Floor, 45 Gee Street	8 W 38th Street, Suite 902	4737/23 Ansari Road
London	New York, NY 10018	Daryaganj
EC1V 3RS	USA	New Delhi 110002
United Kingdom		India

www.koganpage.com

Kogan Page books are printed on paper from sustainable forests.

ISBNs

Hardback	978 1 3986 0829 0
Paperback	978 1 3986 0827 6
Ebook	978 1 3986 0828 3

British Library Cataloguing-in-Publication Data

A CIP record for this book is available from the British Library.

Library of Congress Control Number

2022945057

Typeset by Integra Software Services, Pondicherry
Print production managed by Jellyfish
Printed and bound by CPI Group (UK) Ltd, Croydon, CR0 4YY

Contents

Acknowledgements

No one ever achieves anything alone, and that is most certainly true of writing a book. This book is based on 20 years of research and nearly 40 years of work with teams and leaders from organizations around the world. I have been able to learn from them all, and I hope that they have gained something in return. A few of the firms to which I am indebted are listed below, and my thanks go to all of them.

Accenture, Aegon, AIG, Airbus, ALICO, Allen & Overy, Ambition School Leadership, Amex, ANZ Bank, Apple, Ares & Co, Armstrong Industries, Arrowgrass, AstraZeneca, Aviva, BAML, Bank Indonesia, Barclays, BASF, BNY Mellon, British Council, Canon, Capgemini, Citi, CRU, Dentons, Deutsche Bank, Dow, EBRD, EDS, Education Development Trust, Electrolux, EW Payne, Facebook, Fater, Financial Times, Fujitsu, Gilead Life Sciences, Google, The Groove, HCA, HERE, Hiscox Re, Hitachi, House, HSBC, IBM, Ito Chu, JAL, Laird, Mandarin Capital, MetLife, Mitsubishi Chemical, Mitsui OSK Lines, Mitsui Sumitomo Insurance, Modern Tribe, Monsanto, Nationwide, Nokia, Nomura, Nordea, NRI, NTT, Opportunity Network, Pearson, PepsiCo, Philip Morris, Philips, P&G, Premier Foods, Qualcomm, RBS, RELX, Rentokil, Right to Succeed, Rolls Royce, SABIC, San Miguel, SDP, SECOM, Social Media, Skills Builder, Spark Inside, Standard Chartered Bank, Start Up, STIR, SWIFT, Symantec, Teach First,

Tetrapak, Tokyo Marine, Tui, UBS, Unilever, Vastari, Visa, World Bank, World Faith and Zurich Insurance.

I would in particular like to thank the magnificent team at Kogan Page, led by Helen Kogan. They have always been a joy to work with, and this was no exception. Unusually, the idea for this book came from Kogan Page, not from the author. My thanks to my editor, Chris Cudmore, for commissioning this edition and to Katherine Hartle who worked miracles on revising the text.

Finally, my eternal thanks to my wife, Hiromi, who regularly becomes a book widow for long periods when I am engrossed in writing obsessively. Her patience and support is remarkable.

One theme of this book is that no leader is perfect. The same is true of authors and books: there is no such thing as perfection. Success is always a team effort, but any mistakes are the author's alone.

Introduction

Why this book is needed

Why another book on leadership when there are already nearly 60,000 to choose from? The reason for this book is *because* there are so many books on leadership out there. They all have their theories which fight with each other for your attention. The result is not clarity, but chaos and confusion.

The purpose of this book is to help you find clarity amid the chaos. *Myths of Leadership* is your practical guide to all the myths, fads, theories and fantasies of leadership. It will help you sort out myth from reality and fact from fiction. If leadership is a journey, you need a map. This book is the map which will help you structure your journey and accelerate your path to success, if only by avoiding the many bear traps that exist on the way.

Why this book is different

This book is unusual for three reasons:

1 *It explores not one leadership idea, but 35.* It maps out the entire leadership landscape and highlights some of the traps, dead ends and short cuts you may encounter on your leadership journey.

2 *It is based on three perspectives*, whereas most books are based on just one:

- Twenty years of original leadership research around the world in most industries and countries, as well as research with tribes around the world: truly original insights.

- Forty years of leading, working with and working for great firms and leaders around the world who are recognized in the acknowledgements. In addition, I am a founder or co-founder of eight not-for-profit organizations with a collective turnover above £100 million annually. This means I respect the challenge of leadership in the real world.

- Extensive secondary research, which is needed when investigating myths of leadership. I hope I will have spared you a lot of pain by removing the need for you to read so many books and articles on leadership. Where appropriate, this research is recognized in the notes at the end of each myth.

3 *It offers insight through questions, not answers*. Many leadership books purport to have the secret of leadership wrapped up in three easy steps for you to follow. But real insight does not come from being told something, even if it is true. Real insight comes from discovering something for yourself. So you can treat this book as your journey of discovery through the land of leadership myths. I hope you discover much that you can use and value.

How this book will help

Myths of Leadership does not just deal with myths; it deals with realities. It constantly compares the theory of the myth to the day-to-day reality of leadership. In doing so, it attempts to answer basic questions every leader faces on their journey:

- How do I know if I am really leading: what is a leader?
- Can I lead if I am not the boss?
- Do I need to be charismatic and inspirational to be a leader?
- Can I learn to lead, and if so how?
- Do I need to be visionary or have a vision?
- What must I do to lead well?
- How do I gain the power to lead?

How to use this book

You can read this book in any order you want. You can dip in and out; start at the front and read to the end; or start at the end and work sdrawkcab. Read it all at once, or read just one chapter a day before starting work.

The intent of this book is to provoke thinking about the nature of leadership in general, and about how you can lead better. If the provocation causes you to laugh or curse the book, that is fine. The book does not pretend to have the definitive answer on leadership, because there is no definitive answer on leadership. Instead, it opens new windows on leadership theory and practice and invites you to take a look. You will agree with some perspectives and disagree with others; what you choose to learn from each perspective is up to you.

Throughout the book I attempt to respect most myths, as it is possible to learn something from all of them if we choose to. If we choose to learn nothing, that says something about the myth and something about us. When challenging the myths I have tried, where possible, to provide alternatives. You may feel that these alternatives are themselves myths or that they present reality – that is up to you. They fit broadly into seven major themes:

1 *A leader is someone who takes people where they would not have got by themselves*. Leadership is about what you do, not about your position. You can lead at the bottom of the organization, and you may not be leading even if you are at the top.

2 *Anyone can learn to lead, and everyone can learn to lead better*. Leadership is like playing a sport or a musical instrument – a little practice will make you far better than most people and you can always improve, even if only a few people can become superstars. You do not need to be born a leader.

3 *Leadership is contextual*. There is no universal formula for leadership: there is only what works for you in your context. This means you have to keep on learning and growing because your context keeps on changing. Leadership is a journey, not a destination.

4 *No leader gets ticks in all the boxes*. There is no such thing as a perfect leader, and you do not need to be a charismatic superhuman to lead. You do need some

signature strengths which you can build on and use in a context where you can succeed. Learn to be the best of who you are, rather than attempting to copy some leadership idol.

5 *Leadership is a team sport.* Leaders succeed with other people. They have to build a balanced team which compensates for their weaknesses, has a balance of styles and allows each leader to focus on the one or two things where they can make the most difference. Everything else has to be delegated to the team. Leadership is not about being the lone hero or the Great Man.

6 *Leaders need a vision, but you do not need to be a visionary.* A vision is just a story about how you are going to make a difference. It is a story in three parts: this is where we are, this is where we are going and this is how we will get there. To make it motivational, customize your story to each team member with part four: 'and here is your vital role in helping the team get there'.

7 *Leadership is becoming more challenging.* The core skills required of a leader are growing. In the 19th century, leaders needed intelligence quotient (IQ): bosses had the brains and workers had the hands. An educated workforce in the 20th century could do more but demanded more: leaders needed emotional quotient (EQ) to deal with people. In the 21st century, leaders need to make things happen through people they do not control: they need political quotient (PQ) skills of influencing, building networks of trust and support, aligning agendas and fighting the right battles.

You may find it helpful to refer to this list as you progress through the myths.

Finally, I have attempted to make this book readable. A book on leadership myths is an invitation to get lost in jargon. I have declined that invitation as much as possible. Leadership books can also be pretty dull and pompous (like quite a few people who think they are leaders), so I decided to commit the cardinal sin of attempting to make this book enjoyable to read. In this regard at least, I hope I have sinned successfully on your behalf.

Enjoy the book.

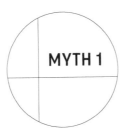

MYTH 1

We know what leadership is

If you want to lead, you have to take people where they would not have got by themselves. That means taking risks, challenging the ways things work today, taking on vested interests and making a real difference.

Defining leadership is like searching for smoke signals in the fog. It can be an exercise in futility. We all think we know what leadership is like, but when we try to agree on a common definition we find ourselves grappling with the fog. This matters because if we cannot agree what leadership is, then judging, discussing or developing leaders becomes impossible. To understand this myth, we will look at leadership from four perspectives.

Common sense

We all know a good leader when we see one: Churchill, Martin Luther King, Nelson Mandela and Mother Theresa. But what about Mao Tse-tung or Stalin: should they be revered as national saviours or reviled as mass murderers? Were they good leaders or not?

We need to define what we mean by a 'good' leader. If good means effective, then we can include many dictators and empire builders down the ages. Alexander the Great was named 'the Great' by the Greeks who were on the winning side. The Persians named him 'Alexander the Barbarian' for destroying their civilization. Being a *good* leader and being an *effective* leader are different concepts.

We can try applying common sense, but common sense can be deeply misleading. It was once common sense to think that the sun rotated around a flat earth; all you had to do was to believe the evidence of your eyes which showed the sun moving through the sky and the world was flat to the horizon.

Common sense seems not to help, so let us turn to practising managers who deal day-to-day with effective and less effective leaders. They should know what leadership is about.

Practising managers

Here is the output of a typical workshop where attendees were asked to define the qualities of a leader:[1]

- ambitious and humble
- directive and empowering

- visionary and practical
- big on ideas and on people
- coaching and controlling
- inspiring, charismatic, authentic and regular

On a good day we might believe that we have all these talents. On most days we will recognize that no one can embody this cornucopia of contradictions.

Successful leaders

It does not help when we look to successful leaders to define leadership. As a research exercise, 100 successful leaders were asked to define leadership.[2] It soon became clear that they were not describing leadership: they were describing themselves. They all assumed that their personal success formula was a universal success formula. But we know that not many leaders succeed when they move into a different industry; great politicians rarely make great business people, and Donald Trump has led many people to believe that the opposite is also true.

If you have the misfortune to read the autobiographies of successful business leaders you will see they fall into the same trap: they think their success formula is a universal one. These autobiographies are particularly dangerous. Anyone who feels the urge to write an autobiography is likely to be a larger-than-life individual interested in their own self-promotion and immortality. Some of these people can be exceptional leaders, but the problem with these exceptional leaders is exactly that: they are exceptional. Most leaders are not like that, and most of us cannot aspire to be like that, even if we wanted to be.

Academic research

This is deeply dangerous territory. Every academic has their own definition of leadership, which they guard jealously. Anyone who argues is likely to suffer the academic equivalent of being burned at the stake for heresy. The challenge for the academic world is that there is no scientific way of establishing what leadership is. There are endless hypotheses, but every hypothesis can be disproven. Even the definitions provided by top thinkers such as Drucker, Kotter and Bennis are inconsistent and do not work:

- Peter Drucker: 'The only definition of a leader is someone who has followers.'[3] This definition fails on two counts:
  - Stars of film, stage and music, and top writers and thinkers like Drucker have followers: that does not make them leaders.
  - Every boss has a team which follows them: just because you are the boss it does not mean you are leading your followers.
- John Kotter: 'Leaders set a direction, align people, motivate and inspire.'[4] This reads well, but does not work. Look closely at each characteristic of Kotter's leader:
  - Leaders may align and motivate people, but don't managers do that as well?
  - Not all leaders are inspirational, even if they are highly effective. You have probably worked for an effective leader without being inspired all the time.
  - That leaders set a direction is closer to the truth, but if the direction is simply a continuation of the past direction, is that leading or following?

- Warren Bennis: 'Managers are people who do things right and leaders are people who do the right thing.'[5] This is a nice aphorism, but the language is better than the thinking. There are plenty of leaders who do catastrophically wrong things. They lead people into the desert, not into the Promised Land. Even leaders who succeed do plenty of things which are wrong: see my point about Stalin and Mao Tse-tung above. The hallmark of most leaders is that they have repeatedly done things wrong, they have failed and they have had the resilience to come back.

Why this myth matters

By now we are in danger of slumping into fashionable postmodern scepticism which holds that there is no truth, there is only what we choose to believe. But if no one has any idea what leadership is, we will struggle to develop leaders. You cannot go on a leadership journey, or any journey, if you do not know what the destination is.

So we need some way forward. We need a working definition of leadership which will allow us to make some progress.

So far, we have looked at the qualities of a good or effective leader. And the result is confusion. So it is time to look at leadership from another perspective. Instead of looking at the qualities of a leader – what they do or what they are – look at what a leader achieves. Looking at what leaders do results in a long and tedious list of activities: leaders motivate people, make decisions, direct resources, breathe and go to the toilet. The list is long because you can always add more activities; it is tedious because it then leads to a debate about which of these activities leaders do and which managers do. It is a debate that leads nowhere. The ultimate focus, therefore, is not on what leaders do or what they are: the focus is on what leaders achieve.

Of all the attempts at defining leadership, the former US Secretary of State Henry Kissinger has probably come closest. He defined a leader as 'someone who takes people where they would not have got by themselves'. This sounds a slightly boring and underwhelming definition of leadership. But it is revolutionary. It cuts through the debate about the qualities of a leader; it differentiates leaders from managers; it shows that leadership is about your performance, not your position. It sets a high bar for leadership, which even the most exalted people often fail to reach.

'Someone who takes people where they would not have got by themselves' is the definition of leadership at the heart of this book. It is a definition which consistently works in practice, if not in theory, but, as Myth 3 demonstrates, there is no theory of leadership which can stand up to scientific challenge. So instead we will have to make do with what works in practice. As we shall see in the following myths, it is a very powerful definition.

Lessons for leaders

If you want to lead, you have to take people where they would not have got by themselves. That means taking risks, challenging the ways things work today, taking on vested interests and making a real difference. Not everyone wants to live and work that way. But for real leaders, it is the only way to live and work.

Here are the top ten consequences of believing that leaders take people where they would not have got by themselves. These points are returned to throughout this book:

1 You can lead at any level. Anyone can learn to lead, and everyone can learn to lead better, even if few of us will become leadership superstars.

2 The person at the top is not necessarily leading: never confuse position with performance.

3 Don't confuse activity with achievement. You may be working very hard, but that does not mean you pass the leadership test. Leaders need to maximize their signal to noise ratio. The signal is how they make a difference; the noise is the day-to-day survival of organizational life, which can consume all your time.

4 Leaders need a clear idea of how things will be different as a result of their leadership. You can call this a mission, vision or strategy if you want to sound important.

5 Leaders require more than formal power to succeed. They need to be able to influence and persuade people they do not control. This becomes more important as firms de-layer and outsource: no one controls all the resources they need to succeed.

6 Leaders do not need to be charismatic and inspirational, but they do need some signature strengths and skills and they need a clear idea of how they will make a difference.

7 No leader has all the skills required to succeed; no one gets ticks in all the boxes. Since you can only excel at what you enjoy, find the context which you will enjoy and where your strengths flourish.

8 Leaders need to build a strong team to deliver for them and to compensate for any weaknesses they may have.

9 Leaders need to build a strong operational machine with effective managers: the leader may lead the revolution, but the leader needs managers to manage the world before, during and after the revolution.

10 Leaders have to keep learning and growing because the context in which they work keeps on changing: what works in one role does not automatically work in the next role.

Ultimately, leadership is like life: it is a voyage of discovery. It may be challenging, but it is rarely dull. It is as good as we want to make it. So whatever your journey is, enjoy it.

Conclusion

One paper found 26,000 academic articles on leadership, which it was able to distil down to 90 variables.[6] That is not a recipe for leadership, it is a recipe for confusion. So the title of this myth is false – we don't seem to be able to agree what leadership is. Most definitions of leadership, including those by top thinkers, don't work. The best I have come across, and the one that this book will follow, is that leaders take people where they would not have got to by themselves.

Notes

1   The author runs regular leadership workshops with clients around the world; this is a typical group response to the question: 'What makes a good leader?'

2   J Owen (2015) *How to Lead*, 4th edn, Pearson, London

3   P Drucker. Your leadership is unique: Good news: there is no one
    'leadership personality', 1996, www.edomi.org/wp-content/
    uploads/2021/01/your-leadership-is-unique-drucker.pdf (archived at
    https://perma.cc/E66A-J225)

4   J P Kotter. What leaders really do, *Harvard Business Review*, 2001,
    79 (11), 85–96

5   W Bennis and B Nanus (1985) *Leaders: The strategies for taking charge*,
    Harper and Row, New York, 21.

6   B E Winston and K Patterson. An integrative definition of leadership,
    International Journal of Leadership Studies, 2016, www.regent.edu/
    acad/global/publications/ijls/new/vol1iss2/winston_patterson.doc/
    winston_patterson.htm (archived at https://perma.cc/J6W6-ZJ2E)

MYTH 2

Leaders need to be perfect

Perfection is not required to lead. No leader gets ticks in all the boxes.

In Myth 1 we saw how followers expect their leaders to be a perfect cornucopia of contradictions:

- ambitious and humble
- directive and empowering
- visionary and practical
- big on ideas and on people
- coaching and controlling
- inspiring, charismatic, authentic and regular

Leaders who think they are this good are well worth avoiding. For the rest of us, this is a daunting list.

Human resources (HR) systems do not help much either. They also come up with a long list of talents and capabilities which we have to master. How can we achieve perfection in such an imperfect world?

THE PERFECT PREDATOR

It had been a hard research trip with the Pokot and Turkana tribes in northern Kenya. On the way back to Nairobi we went through Samburu National Park. We saw lots of wild animals and started to have an argument about who was the king of the jungle (or, more accurately, the hills and plains). Some favoured the lion, others the crocodile who feared no one, and some the elephant because all animals give way to elephants at a water hole.

We decided to settle the argument by creating the true king of the jungle: the perfect predator. We all took responsibility for one limb. The result was a beast with the jaws of a crocodile, the ears of an elephant, the neck of a giraffe, the hide of a rhino, the tail of a scorpion and the legs of the cheetah. The animal promptly died under the weight of its own improbability.

The same is true of leaders. The perfect leader is not a mix of all the best bits of every leader who has ever breathed air. The perfect leader is the one who fits the context. The lion thrives on the plains and would not last long in the Arctic where the reindeer rule; a reindeer on the Serengeti would be called 'lunch'. If you want to lead, find the context where you will succeed.

Why this myth matters

In life there is often a gap between what we want and what we get. This is true of our leaders. We want leaders who are perfect and we end up with [you can name your favourite politicians or bosses here].

As your leadership journey progresses, you will find that you slowly move out of the shadows and into the limelight. In time you might take centre stage, with the spotlight and cameras on you picking up every detail of what you do and every nuance of what you say. Life in the shadows is hard but forgiving. Any minor weaknesses (or 'development opportunities' in HR speak) will only be seen by the people closest to you. When you are centre stage, every minor blemish and every misstep is magnified 100-fold and is seen by everyone. The result is that we see the weaknesses of our leaders very clearly. We know that they are not perfect, and in our hearts we know they never can be.

This is exceptionally good news for all leaders. It means that perfection is not required to lead. No leader gets ticks in all the boxes.

Lessons for leaders

The most important lesson is one of hope: you do not need to be perfect to succeed. Besides this inspirational lesson, there are five practical lessons which will help you on your leadership journey to success, not perfection.

1. Chase fit, not perfection

Instead of perfection, you have to seek fit. You either have to develop the talents to suit your context or you have to find the context to suit your talents. The latter is more effective than the former; it is easier to change your context than to change your talents.

2. Build on your strengths

Everyone has a few signature strengths, which can be anything from being deeply analytical or creative, to being highly effective working in teams. These strengths are the fuel for your leadership journey; make sure you find the context where they are vital to success, and you will flourish.

3. Work around your weaknesses

Corporate development systems often require you to work on your weaknesses. This is catastrophic advice. Weightlifters do not win in the Olympics by working on their weakness in synchronized swimming. If you are highly analytical but less creative, you will not succeed by trying to become the creative heart of your firm. You can work around your weaknesses in three ways:

- Avoid working in contexts where your weaknesses are the key skills required. Find the context where you and your strengths flourish.
- Build a team which is strongest where you are weakest. If you hate bookkeeping, love bookkeepers: they can do what you prefer not to.

- Learn enough to ensure that your weakness is not fatal, but do not try to turn it into a strength.

4. Keep on learning

Leadership is a journey, not a destination. The nature of your leadership challenge keeps on changing, at each level of the firm (see Myth 8) and with each assignment. When the context changes, you have to change. This is what makes the leadership journey so fulfilling and exciting: enjoy the ride.

5. Avoid the prison of success

Success can be lethal to a career. Many leaders fail because they have huge success in one context. This then becomes their success formula, which they want to apply to every situation. But not every problem is solved with a hammer; you need different tools and different approaches for different situations. The prison of success is the prison of your past. Avoid it.

Conclusion

The perfect leader is completely mythical. It makes leadership seem unattainable for mere mortals. But this is good news for leaders. You do not need to be perfect.

MYTH 3

We have a theory about leadership

There is no single unifying theory of leadership.
No one can agree what leaders are like, what leaders
should do or even what leadership is.

Leadership gives rise to an endless conveyer belt of new theories, all of which promise to help leaders succeed. These theories promise to give insights into what leaders are like, the qualities they need, and what leaders should do to make a difference. They also vary widely: there is no single unifying theory of leadership. No one can agree what leaders are like, what leaders should do or even what leadership is.

No leadership theory stands up to any form of scientific test for long, because every theory can be quickly falsified. There is no universal formula for leadership like $E = mc^2$.

But every leadership theory has some value; it opens a new window on reality and invites us to think again about what really works and does not work.

Theories of leadership

This myth touches on seven of the most widely known theories of leadership which have existed for varying degrees of time. Some are now largely discredited, but that doesn't mean they are useless. We can learn from any theory if we use choose to. Each of these theories could be a myth in its own right.

Great Man theory of leadership

This theory has its origins in the 19th-century belief that 'the history of the world is but the biography of great men'.[1] This made for gripping history: it was the history of heroes achieving great things and changing the course of mankind. It was the sort of history which could inspire generations of schoolchildren.

There was just one small problem with this approach to history: it was wrong. The counter argument, put by Herbert Spencer, was that great men do not make society; society makes the man: 'Before the Great Man can remake his society, his society must make him.'[2] This put the primacy of economics, society and technology at the heart of history. Karl Marx made an early attempt to explain history through the force of economics and society. Since then, the practice of history has become more professional and the deep forces of economics and society have become better, if imperfectly, understood.

The Great Man theory of history lives on as the Great Man theory of leadership. The idea is that the leader changes the destiny of a business through sheer will of leadership. The belief is that leaders (great men) can reshape the future. As evidence for the Great Man theory of leadership we have the billionaire entrepreneurs of today: we owe Microsoft, Google, Apple, Facebook and other breakthrough firms to the driving force of their founders. And most of the great firms of today, from Ford to Sony to Toyota, were founded by great visionaries who conjured their businesses out of the thin air of imagination and courage. The question is whether these entrepreneurs shape the world or are simply products of the time they live in.

The counter argument is that businesses are shaped by their times. The evidence for this is the survival rate of the top firms. The life expectancy of a Fortune 500 company was 61 years in 1958 and is now less than 18 years. Seventy-five per cent of firms in the index today will not be in it in ten years' time, according to McKinsey projections.[3]

This theory is largely discredited and dangerous to the practice of leadership: you do not need to be great or male to lead, and nations and firms are in trouble when they look for a hero to save them. Destiny, in the form of economics, society and technology, shapes the nature of businesses which rise or fall. Leaders make sure their business is the one that makes the most of destiny.

The Great Man theory is useful insofar as it is a call to action. It challenges leaders to shape events rather than be shaped by them. You may not change the destiny of the world, but you can change the destiny of your team. Leaders believe they can control, or at least influence, events; victims believe they are controlled by events.

Servant leadership

Traditional leadership involves a leader accumulating and exercising power over people and other resources. The idea of servant leadership runs in the opposite direction. The servant leader is not the ruler, but the server. They serve two things:

1 the mission
2 the organization

This myth became fashionable in business circles early in this millennium. Chief executive officers (CEOs) often liked to present themselves as the servant leader by inverting the organization pyramid. The idea was to show that the most important people in the firm are the front-line workers who make things, move things, sell things or deal with customers. The job of leadership and management was simply to support front-line staff.

This theory was very much a fad and didn't last. It was not inspirational, but cringe-making. The CEO may have believed their speech about being less important than people on the front line, but it didn't wash with the audience. The upside-down pyramid looked like a spinning top out of control. And if the CEO was really that unimportant, how could their pay cheque be justified?

When it comes to serving the mission, leaders might start with this intention but slowly the mission comes to serve them. It becomes a vehicle for promoting themselves and building their profile and prestige. They might remain passionate about the mission, but only because it serves them so well. This is a subtle change which staff notice, and it leads to hubris and eventually nemesis.

This theory serves as a useful lesson to avoid management fads. They may look and sound great, but they need to reflect reality. Like all the greatest fads and myths, servant leadership is a mountain of nonsense built on a kernel of truth. There are some notable true servant leaders who are honourable and successful, but they are the exceptions that prove the rule.

The humble leader

The idea of the humble leader is a reaction to the Great Man theory of leadership – it's pretty much the opposite of being a Great Man. There is no set and agreed definition of what a humble leader is. Different people project different qualities onto the humble leader, to suit their needs and opinions.

There appear to be three themes to humility:

1 *Humble about self*

There are benefits associated with being humble about yourself. It makes you more inclusive, encourages you to recognize others for their strengths and make sure you are consistently learning and growing. But there are also downsides. It can be taken to mean that leaders have to admit their failings, weaknesses, doubts and shortcomings in public. This is taken to be authentic leadership (see below) which humanizes leaders and makes them more approachable. This takes humility too far. Leaders are dealers in hope. They should craft a positive vision for their team. If instead they mumble about their fears, doubts and weaknesses their team might doubt their ability to lead.

2 *Humble with others*

   Humility leads to more engaged teams. This has been proved even in China, which is traditionally seen as a very hierarchical society.[4] But this is only true up to a point. All things being equal, a more engaged team will perform better than a less engaged team. But all things are never equal. There is a downside to humility, and that is lack of ambition.

3 *Humble in terms of ambition*

   This is the dark side of humility. Humble leaders are less likely to challenge the system, force change or build a compelling vision. If you underappreciate your own talents, and defer to the skills of others, you are unlikely to be the revolutionary leader who takes people where they would not have got to by themselves.

Distributed leadership

This is a reinvention of a very old idea which addresses an eternal problem: how do you lead across a system which is complex and dispersed? Like many of the theories here, it kicks back against the idea of the leader being a Great Man or Great Woman. The theory suggests that leadership can be shared among a group, rather than relying on one person.

It is highly relevant in a global context where there is tension between maintaining central control and distributing power to teams around the world. Making global teams work highlights the challenges of putting this theory into practice. The trade-off between control and delegation is at the heart of distributed leadership. To delegate confidently, you need trust your team and have effective control mechanisms in place.

Distributed leadership is not really a theory of leadership. It is a reality of leadership. I write more about distributed leadership in Myth 14.

Transactional and transformational leadership

These are linked theories which originated in the 1970s. Debates raged at conferences over the merits of transformational leadership over transactional leadership. The debate followed the true dialectic tradition of Marx and Hegel,[5] in which a thesis (transformational leadership) generated an antithesis (transactional leadership) which led to a synthesis: you need a bit of both. Whether the leaders of the capitalist world saw themselves following a Marxist tradition is questionable.

The two theories follow two fundamentally different approaches. Transformational leadership focuses on having a strong vision and mission, and bringing your team along with you to achieve that mission. Transformational leaders are charismatic and inspirational. They motivate their followers to pursue change (see Myth 9).

In contrast, transactional leadership focuses on building an organization machine which works. The leader's focus should be on establishing clear goals, rewards and sanctions which appeal to the self-interest of each team member. They maintain the status quo, rather than challenging it as transformational leaders do. Rather than being motivational and focusing on influencing your team members, transactional leaders are organized, analytical, objective and fair. Teams are self-interested and utilitarian: they seek to maximize pleasure and minimize pain.

Transactional leadership works well in an immediate crisis where the focus is on survival. It also works where people have relatively low engagement with their work and simply want to know what they need to do.

Transformational leadership can work for professionals who do not want to be micro-managed, but in reality it expects too much from the leader. Lifting your team to a higher moral purpose is nice, but it is neither necessary nor doable.

The reality is that leaders need to be transformational *and* transactional; they have to manage people and tasks; they have to motivate and control. It is not either/or: leaders have to do it all.

Authentic leadership

Authentic leadership is a slippery theory. There is no agreed version of what it is. Two traits appear consistently in discussions about the theory:

1 A leader has to be true to who they are.
2 Authentic leaders are open about their thoughts and beliefs.

From these twin pillars, people add whatever else they want onto the idea of an authentic leader: someone who solicits feedback, is fair minded, has a strong ethical foundation. In other words, 'authentic' is a code word for 'ideal'. The broader the definition becomes, the less useful it is.

Myth 17 considers the side of authentic leadership that states a leader is open about their thoughts and beliefs. Here we'll consider the first point: that a leader has to be true to who they are.

At one level, this is a truism which challenges much of leadership literature. There are many books which claim to hold the secrets of everyone from Genghis Khan to Steve Jobs. But you cannot succeed by trying to be someone else.

Equally, if you try to be yourself you will fail. If you hang around like a teenager waiting for the world to recognize your true genius, you'll have a very long wait. So we have a paradox.

The resolution is simple: leaders have to become the best of who they are. You cannot pretend to be someone you are not. Nor can you become someone else. Fortunately, leadership is a team sport. You can and should build your team so that it has a balance of skills, styles and strengths. Find team members who can fill in for areas which are not your strengths.

But it is not enough to just be who you are. Every leader has one or two signature strengths. Find yours and build on them. Find roles and firms where your strengths are in demand because that is where you will flourish.

Leadership is a team sport

Leadership is no longer about the Great Man and lone hero leading the multitude to a sunny future. Business is too complicated and changes too fast for any one person to master. And 'the multitude' are no longer poorly educated masses who have few choices in life. They are more likely to be highly educated professionals who expect to be involved in shaping their future. In this new context, leadership has to be a team sport rather than an individual one.

In theory, team leadership makes sense. It enables the full creativity and power of the team to be unleashed; it enables different talents to flourish and it reduces the risk of depending on one person. In practice, leadership fails to follow the theory; leadership teams often act as a group of individuals rather than a team. Meetings are more like a series of table tennis matches between the chair and each person sitting around the table. Each business unit or function serves up a few proposals; the chair bats back a few questions and challenges. There are three reasons for this:

1 Rational – responsibility can be shared, but account-ability cannot, which means that each business unit or function has to answer for its own performance.
2 Political – there is a rule of survival at board level: keep your nose out of other people's business. While it might be tempting to offer your views on you colleagues' failings, this can invite nuclear-scale retaliation.
3 Emotional – bosses like to boss. It is relatively easy to deal with board members one at a time. It's much harder to control the outcome of an open discussion.

When building a leadership team, there's a trade-off between creating a team and creating a group of individu-als. This comes down to balancing accountability and responsibility. The theory behind leadership as a team sport makes sense, but reality has a pesky habit of not living up to the theory.

Why this myth matters

The comparative length of this myth reflects the wide variety of leadership theories. This variety is very good news for leaders. If there was a single formula for leadership, leaders would soon be following the fate of Korean baseball fans, camel racing jockeys and dairy hands: we could all be replaced by robots.[6] The fact that there are so many leadership theories shows that leadership remains more of an art than a science.

Lessons for leaders

Avoid too much theory. It is easy to drown in the ocean of leadership theory. Your job is to master leadership, not leadership theory.

That being said, there is a surprising lesson for leaders from these theories: they can all help. While no leadership theory offers a universal truth, all leadership theories offer some insight.

Conclusion

There is no one theory of leadership. You do not have to slavishly follow a set of leadership rules. You can find your own way to lead; there are countless ways to succeed or to fail. This makes the leadership journey endlessly challenging and rewarding. All theories can help, if you use them well. Use them as a call to action and tailor the implementation to your needs and situation.

Notes

1   T Carlyle (1840) The hero as divinity, *On Heroes, Hero-Worship and the Heroic in History*, various editions

2   T Hobbes (1651) *Leviathan*, Oxford University Press, Oxford

3   S Garelli. Why you will probably live longer than most big companies, IMD, 2016, www.content.imd.org/research-knowledge/articles/why-you-will-probably-live-longer-than-most-big-companies/ (archived at https://perma.cc/PW6D-GMC4)

4   A Y Ou, A S Tsui, A J Kinicki, D A Waldman, Z Xiao and L J Song. Humble chief executive officers' connections to top management team integration and middle managers' responses, *Administrative Science Quarterly*, 2014, 59 (1), 34–72

5   Marx argued that his form of dialectical materialism contradicted Hegel's dialectics. Never get in the middle of an argument between two philosophers.

6   A struggling Korean baseball team tried to solve the problem of its lack of support by installing robot fans in the stalls: www.youtube.com/watch?v=PHTK63fgl4M (archived at https://perma.cc/CV7T-ADDC); camel racing is enjoying a resurgence in the UAE, with robots riding the camels: www.youtube.com/watch?v=pDBGdEZa9eM (archived at https://perma.cc/A2NR-3MN7); T Heyden. The cows that queue up to milk themselves, BBC, 2015, www.bbc.co.uk/news/magazine-32610257 (archived at https://perma.cc/L9TM-AXA4)

MYTH 4

Leadership is about your rank, title or position

Never confuse position with performance.

Organizations are hierarchies. This leads to a fatal mistake: everyone assumes that their boss is the leader. Even in the largest and most prestigious firms, you can ask a group of senior executives who is the leader, and they will all point to their boss.

Why this myth matters

The myth is dangerous for two reasons.

Having a grand title does not make you a leader

It simply means you have a grand title. There are plenty of CEOs, presidents and prime ministers who failed to lead: they simply administered a legacy they inherited. There is nothing wrong with managing a legacy. As a good steward of a legacy you should hope to leave the legacy better than when you found it. This was explained well by the CEO of the Grosvenor Group, which is over 300 years old. His job was not to transform the ancient property company into a glorious high-tech firm that would go bust; his job was to manage the legacy for future generations. This is the art of management, and it is much underrated. But it is not leadership.

A leader has to take people where they would not have got by themselves. As an exercise, think of how many presidents or prime ministers you can recall who succeeded in taking the country in a new direction, and a direction they intended to go in. Most of these famous people fail. When I do this exercise with groups in the UK, only two prime ministers out of 18 since 1945 pass the test: Attlee founded the Welfare State, and Thatcher gave us the word Thatcherism. All the others are remembered for trivia or mistakes.

Just because you have the big title, that does not mean you are a leader. Never confuse position with performance. Leadership is about what you do, not what your title is. This gives the clue to the second reason the myth is dangerous.

Having a boss does not stop you from leading

If leadership is about what you do, not about your title, then you can lead wherever you are in the firm. You do not have to lead people to the Promised Land to be a leader. If you change the way your service team works, you are taking people where they would not have got by themselves: you are leading.

You will never reach the corner office unless you learn to lead from an early stage. You have to show that you can make a difference. Fortunately, there are always opportunities to grow your leadership capabilities. In every firm, there are moments of uncertainty, doubt and ambiguity; there are crises and new opportunities where no one is sure what to do. These are the moments of truth when leaders step up and followers step back.

PASSING THE LEADERSHIP TEST

Duncan was the facilities manager. This is the role where everyone ignores you or moans at you. They moan about the catering, the furniture, the lighting, the toilets, the flowers, the car parking, the signage: you name it, it is your fault if you are the facilities manager.

So how can you be a leader if you are the lowly facilities manager?

One day, the partners of the firm went to their global meeting. Duncan was not invited, but he heard the senior partner had made a big speech about working as teams and being more customer focused. It was the sort of standard speech that everyone ignores. But Duncan chose not to ignore it.

Duncan decided to approach the senior partner, which meant going to the office with the deep carpet and reproduction antiques which Duncan had supplied. He was ushered into the presence of the senior partner.

Duncan laid out his idea. 'If you really want teamwork, we will have to get rid of all the private offices and little cubicles, and go open plan... which should save a lot of money.' Working from home will save us even more money. The partner smiled, so Duncan carried on: 'Of course, that means leadership will have to set an example: the senior partners will need to start by sharing an office.' The partner's smile evaporated: he had been caught. He could not say 'no' but did not want to say 'yes'.

Duncan then carried on: 'In practice we need only about 70 desks for every 100 staff. We should get as many staff out working with clients: more client focus and less cost to us.' The senior partner began to wonder who he had hired as facilities manager.

Duncan may have been a manager by title, but he was a leader by action. He was actively taking the firm where it would not have got by itself. He was even leading the senior partner. Duncan persuaded the senior partner to do something he would never have done by himself.

Lessons for leaders

This myth is bittersweet. There are different lessons for you, depending where you are in the hierarchy:

- If you are at the top of the firm, do not assume that means you are leading. Being at the top simply means you have a big title and perhaps a big salary. If you want to lead, you will have to show that you are taking the firm where it would not have got by itself.
- If you are at the top of the firm, do not feel the need to be a transformational leader. Being a good steward of a

legacy you inherited is worthwhile if you want the firm to survive for 300 years.

- If you are in the middle or junior ranks of management, that should not stop you from thinking and acting as a leader. Inevitably, most of your time will be spent on management tasks, because that will be your job. But within your job, you should find opportunities to re-shape how your section operates; you may even find a chance to change the wider firm.

- Thinking and acting like a leader does not start when you reach the 'corner office'. By then it is too late: you will already have the habits of a lifetime which will con-dition how you act. That means that if you want to lead, you have to start thinking and acting as a leader from the earliest stage.

Leadership is about performance, not position. You can lead whatever your title is. You can be at the top of the firm and not leading; you can be at the bottom of the firm and be a leader. Your choice. Choose well.

Conclusion

This myth cuts to the heart of the leadership debate and overturns the lazy assumption that the boss is a leader. It challenges those at the top and liberates those at the bottom to be real leaders.

MYTH 5

Managers are leaders

*Leaders may change the world, but managers
run the world.*

We live in a world of word inflation. If you get one song into the charts, you get billed as a global megastar. The old personnel department has become the strategic human capital division. Sales people are now relationship managers. Traders at banks become vice presidents with no one reporting to them. And nowadays, all managers are told that they are really leaders.

The debate about the difference between a leader and a manager can quickly become a matter of opinion which generates more heat than light.

Fortunately, I have discovered that there is one statistically proven difference between leadership and management – leadership sells more books. I have written books on leadership and books on management. Books with 'Lead' in the title outsell books with 'Manage' in the title by about five to one. This is true across all business books: mentioning the word 'leader' instead of 'manager' boosts sales dramatically. We all want to be leaders, not managers.

Why this myth matters

At one level, there is no harm in title inflation; it is a cheap way of recognizing people who work hard and make a serious contribution. But at another level, it does matter because the cult of leadership undervalues both leadership and management, and is a source of mismatched expectations.

Undervaluing leadership

One major retail chain is proud of the fact that its new graduates on the shop floor act like real leaders: they have to find solutions to staffing shortages, they have to keep maintaining high standards on store cleanliness and stock availability, and they have to deal with an endless variety of customer situations. There is no doubt that this a highly demanding set of tasks for a recent graduate, but is it leadership? If that is what leaders do, then what are all the top management doing?

This is where the Kissinger definition of leadership helps: 'Leaders take people where they would not have got by themselves.' This makes it clear that much of what is deemed to be 'leadership' is not leadership at all: it is highly effective management.

Revolutions provide an insight into the nature of leadership. Revolutions need revolutionary leaders who will upset the old order and bring in the new world of hope, prosperity and fairness – although some revolutions seem to bring gulags and dictatorship. But before and after the revolution you need countless managers who make sure that the trains run on time and that the bread gets delivered each morning. If your revolution is all leaders and no managers you have chaos. Leaders may change the world, but managers run the world.

By assuming that all managers are leaders, we undervalue leadership. Leadership is a high bar to jump.

Undervaluing management

The modern fetish with leadership means that no one wants to be seen as a 'mere' manager. Why be a manager when you can be a leader? This seriously undervalues both the importance and challenge of being a great manager.

As we have seen with the revolutions analogy, you need managers to run the world before, during and after the revolution. Managers enable great leaders to lead; without good management, a leader can talk much and achieve little.

The challenge of management is, if anything, even greater than the challenge of leadership. Managers lack the control and clarity available to leaders:

- Leaders normally have control over the resources they need to achieve their goals; every year managers find that their budget goes down but their targets go up.
- Leaders have the authority to match their responsibility; standard operating practice for managers is to have

responsibilities which exceed their authority. They have to find ways of influencing people over whom they have no control to make things happen. Staff functions often seem to help the CEO, but hinder other managers.

- Leaders have control over their direction: they decide where to go. Managers in the middle often find themselves facing conflicting demands from different parts of the organization. They have to resolve the ambiguity that is inherent to the middle of any firm.

Managers have to make things happen through other people. It is seriously hard work. Success is not natural because events always conspire against managers: staff leave; suppliers let you down; customers want more for less; the taxman just wants more and top management bring forward deadlines and come up with bright ideas for you to act on.

Instead of pretending that all managers are leaders, we should celebrate managers for what they are: the backbone of success in any organization.

Mismatched expectations

Graduate recruiters will always hype up their offering. A standard part of the hype is to show that they expect their newly minted employees to act like leaders from the start. These new leaders then find themselves consigned to doing boring grunt work which is the staple of all people learning a new trade. The expectations mismatch is a major source of frustration and helps to drive large turnover of staff in the early years of their career. Cheap talk can be very expensive.

Lessons for leaders

- *Do a reality check: are you really leading?* If you are a manager, celebrate that. Your work is the bedrock of success for any firm.
- *Celebrate and value your managers.* You are only as good as your management team. They are the people that will turn ideas into reality.
- *Set expectations clearly.* Not everyone can be leading all the time. Even the best leaders spend most of their time on management tasks: making things run and avoiding disaster, rather than changing the world. If you value management properly, then no one will have a problem being called a manager and they will understand what they have to do. If you pretend everyone is going to be a leader from day one, you will find you have many frustrated and disappointed managers who will look for greener pastures elsewhere.

Conclusion

This is a myth which manages to devalue both leadership and management. We should value management more, and understand how leadership is different.

MYTH 6

The founder is the leader

The job of the founder is not to be the smartest person on the team; it is to get the smartest people onto the team.

The essence of this myth is based on a simple reality: the easiest way to lead something is to start something. The question is whether the founder is the right person to lead, and for how long.

You don't have to found a firm to be a founder. Within a firm, if you start a new initiative, you are the founder of that idea. If you found something within a firm, then the idea of the founder as leader principle works well.

The founder as leader appears natural when founding a new firm. Like volcanoes, crocodiles and hurricanes, what is natural can be very dangerous. Within a firm, if you have an idea you will normally get first shot at making the idea happen. First mover advantage is very powerful. Once you are leading the new project, or developing the new product, all sorts of people will come on board and make a difference. But they are all fine-tuning the big idea you started with. Within the firm, you have to keep on earning the right to lead your idea. If you start to struggle you will first receive support and then you will be replaced. The founder's rights are strictly limited; you get a chance to lead, but you do not get freehold leadership rights for your idea.

A big challenge arises with founders of firms and not-for-profits, who will often have a stranglehold on governance through shareholdings or through the membership structure of the not-for-profit. The normal checks and balances that exist within the firm do not apply to the founder of the firm. They can go on until they are making billions or until they go bust.

The problem gets worse as a result of survivor bias. We all read the tales of brilliant entrepreneurs who start in the mythical garage and land up jetting around the world meeting presidents and addressing the World Economic Forum. This gives the illusion that the founder is always the person who has to lead the firm to success. We never hear about those who do not survive; they started in the garage, built up a small business and then went bust. For every founder who becomes a billionaire there are countless thousands of founders who do not make the grade. The job of the founder is not to be the smartest person on the team; it is to get the smartest people onto the team.

Why this myth matters

This myth matters because the founder is not always the right person to lead their business, but they often find it very difficult to let go. When you start a new venture, it is your baby; you put all your time and effort into making it succeed. The thought of handing over to someone else is anathema; they might kill your baby or turn it into a monster. And for many entrepreneurs, the joy is in the journey. It is not just about making money, although that helps; it is about the joy of turning an idea into reality.

There is magic in creating something out of nothing, and no founder wants to give up that magic. At a more prosaic level, founders know that they have limited options. They know that trying to start another successful start-up is hazardous at best. And they also know that they cannot return to working for someone else. Founding a firm is a one-way leap: once you have tasted the freedom and terror of starting your own business it is emotionally impossible to return to the gilded cage of employment. The petty rules, the politics, the indignity of working for someone you do not respect are hard to deal with.

Founders often struggle to lead their start-up to maturity for the same reason that young leaders within a firm find it hard to become middle and senior leaders. Whether you work inside a firm or you have started a firm the rules of leadership success change as you progress. Within the firm, you are likely to move more slowly and receive more support. When you start a new firm, growth can be dramatic and you lack the support infrastructure to help you learn and lead.

When you start a new business, you are your own sales force, customer management, head of operations, IT help desk, HR department and facilities manager. You have to do everything, and it is massively inefficient. Transitioning from there into a large organization which has its own IT, operations, finance and accounting, HR, legal, sales and marketing is a huge leap. If you are doing all these things yourself, you are a founder but not a leader. As a leader, you have to build the team which will turn your idea into reality. If you do that, you will have succeeded as a leader and entrepreneur, regardless of what title you give yourself. Never confuse your title and your role: you do not have to be the CEO to be the leader.

Lessons for leaders

Move first, move fast

Founders within a firm benefit hugely from first mover advantage. You will normally get the chance to lead your idea if you are first to move. This is true of moments of crisis and ambiguity when no one is quite sure what to do, or all the options seem too risky. First mover advantage also applies to start-ups, many of which are team efforts. Be part of the founding team, which normally means getting involved before there is a website, name or legal entity. If you are involved that early, you have the chance to shape your destiny. If you join later, you will find that your destiny is shaped by the first movers: the founding team.

Know where you add value

As a founder you will bring some magic sauce to the firm you start. You will have the inspiration, passion and vision. This makes you the natural cheerleader-in-chief in dealing with customers, investors and partners. You may also have some specific talent to bring. As founder, you have the right to shape your role as you want it, and that does not mean you have to be CEO.

Build your team

Focus on what you can do well, and bring in other talent to support you. You would not consider doing all your own bookkeeping as the firm grows because other people can do that better: apply the same principle to all the management and leadership tasks of the firm.

Learn and grow fast

If you want to lead the firm to scale, you need to learn and adapt fast. See Myth 8 for how the skills of leadership change at each level of the firm. You will not be progressing in terms of seniority, but you will be progressing in terms of scale. Scale is a good proxy for seniority: the larger your business, the more your leadership role looks like a senior role.

Conclusion

Starting something is the easiest way to lead something, which means that this is in danger of being reality, not myth. But many founders fail because they are not good leaders. All good myths mix truth and fantasy. This is no exception.

MYTH 7

Leadership is universal

Instead of trying to build cultural knowledge, build cultural intelligence.

Amazon offer more than 60,000 books with the word 'leadership' in their title. With this book, you can add one more to the total. Happy reading.

Like latter-day alchemists, most of these books attempt to find the elixir of leadership. Most offer some useful insight into leadership, but the quest for universal truth is as pointless as the medieval quest for the elixir of eternal youth, or the formula for turning base metal into gold. There is no universal formula; there is only what works for you in your context. One of the critical dimensions of context is global; different cultures lead and manage in different ways.

Because most of the leadership literature is written in English by writers from the English-speaking world, there is a heavy bias towards assuming that the Anglo way is the right way. In the era of American hegemony, there was some justification to this. It meant that globalization was the code word for spreading western practices around the world. The rise of Japan and its decimation of various western industries was the first wake-up call. The second wake-up call is the rise of China and the rest of Asia.

Despite this, leadership still has a strong Western bias. As one Japanese manager put it: 'We read many business books by American authors, but how many Americans have read business books by Japanese authors?' The Japanese understand America better than Americans understand Japan. Indeed, the greatest success of Japanese management was the deployment of the Quality Movement. They had learned the principles of quality from an American, W Edwards Deming,[1] but America only adopted Deming's methods when Japan started its onslaught.

The world understands the West, but does the West understand the world? There is a huge knowledge gap between East and West, which is not to the advantage of the West.

Why this myth matters

Leadership varies around the world. You cannot assume that what works in one culture will work in another.[2]

Table 7.1 highlights a few of the differences between a few of the cultures. Research has shown that even when you make the very short trip by train under the Channel Tunnel from the UK to France, all the rules change.[3] The following vignette makes the point.

ANGLO–FRENCH COLLABORATION AND CONFLICT

Bertrand was *Chef de Cabinet*: he led a large government ministry in Paris. During our interview, he mentioned that the British are very pragmatic decision makers. That sounded like a compliment, but he is French and I am British, so it had to be an insult. I asked Bertrand to explain:

'In France we are very rigorous in decision making. We take an intellectual approach, so when we arrive at a decision we know it is right and we stick with it. But you are more pragmatic: you do what makes sense today, but tomorrow you might change your mind. And because you don't use body language, we don't know what you are thinking. So we don't know what you think but we do know you will change your mind. So that is why we find it hard to trust the Brits.'

I probably looked crestfallen, because then he added helpfully: 'But don't worry, the Germans are worse...'.

Lessons for leaders

Build your cultural intelligence

There is a huge amount of literature out there which maps the cultural differences between nations, but no one can master all the cultural nuances of the world. Your job is not to be an anthropologist; your job is to lead. The principles are easy, even if the practice is hard:

- *Don't assume that your way is the right way.* One reason for global working is to find the best talent and best solutions in the world.

- *Be quick to observe, learn and adapt.* Stay curious: try the local foods, music and ways of doing things. Working globally is a great chance to broaden your experience and capabilities, so make the most of it.
- *Recognize that you are the one with the exotic culture and habits.* See the text box *Who has the exotic culture?*
- *Have positive regard.* On global teams, misunderstandings arise more easily and are harder to fix. When this happens, assume the other side is professional and wants to do a good job. Avoid suspicion and the blame game.
- *Communication starts with understanding.* This means listening more than you talk.

WHO HAS THE EXOTIC CULTURE?

It was late and we were drunk. That is the point in the evening in Japan when you can tell the truth and still be forgiven in the morning. The senior executive leaned over to me and said, 'Jo-san: there is something I need to ask you.' I leaned in towards him: we were clearly getting down to business.

'How do you shake hands?' he asked.

We think Japanese bowing is impenetrable. It is not. *Meishi* (business cards) give you all the information you need to know who should bow first, deepest and longest: that is why *meishi* are always exchanged immediately on first meetings.

By comparison, shaking hands is a mystery. What are the rules? When do you know to shake hands and with whom? How hard and how long do you shake? Are the rules the same everywhere? And let's not even get onto the French habit of kissing...

Now you try to explain the rules of shaking hands.

TABLE 7.1 Leadership and business styles in four cultures

Factor	UK	Japan	Traditional societies	France
Decision processes	Pragmatic, well communicated	Consensual	Communal, open	Top down, well thought through
Hierarchy	Call boss by first name	Respect-based language	Age and sex	Tu, vous, title depending on relationship
Networks	Based on profession	Based on keiretsu	Family based	Academic background
Education focus	Liberal arts	Maths, science, engineering	Informal, oral, generalists	Maths and science
Key industries	City, services, media	Engineering, manufacturing	Subsistence	Engineering, luxury goods
Values	Ethics, spirit of the law	Honesty and trust, outside law	Respect for the community	Honesty, letter of the law
Delegation	Responsibility exceeds authority	Collective responsibility	Compartmentalization of roles	Responsibility requires authority
Feedback	Indirect, often positive	Avoided	No	Direct, often negative
Body language	Hidden, appears devious	Formality, ritual	Open	Open and direct
Openness	Wimbledonization of London	Closed	Binary	Closed: revolution not evolution
Law	Common law, flexible	Avoid using law	Tradition, personal	Roman law, highly prescriptive
Thinking	Pragmatic	Practical	Tradition	Theoretical, based on principles
Meetings	Make decisions	Confirm decisions	Social	Air views, defend position

Source J Owen (2007) *Tribal Business School*, Wiley, Chichester

Conclusion

This myth is widespread and dangerous at every level. Individuals think that their success formula is unique, and then fail when they are in a new context. The West thinks it has a monopoly on wisdom, but is being challenged by leaders who think differently.

Notes

1 W Edwards Deming (2000) *Out of the Crisis*, MIT Press, Cambridge, MA

2 J Owen (2016) *Global Teams*, Pearson, London

3 P Walker. Crossing the Anglo–French divide, CNN, 2007, http://edition.cnn.com/2007/BUSINESS/04/30/execed.anglofrench/ (archived at https://perma.cc/HU6P-DQYS)

We know what leaders do

*Leadership is contextual. There
is no one-size-fits-all leader.*

At one level we know exactly what leaders do. They talk to people, they listen, they send emails, have meetings and read documents. But that is what anyone does in an office job. We can also see that leaders breathe: true, but useless. The real question is: 'Do we know what leaders do, that no one else does?' There is no single, simple answer to that question. In different contexts, leaders do different things. For instance, leaders who grow the firm and leaders who cut costs are very different beasts: they have different skills and will do different things.

This means that leadership is contextual. There is no one-size-fits-all leader. Different leaders are needed for different challenges, and when your context changes, the nature of leadership changes. This is particularly true when you gain promotion. This myth is implicitly recognized in most firms' appraisal and development processes: you are expected to perform differently in different roles and at different levels.

Why this myth matters

This matters for two reasons:

1 appointing leaders
2 managing your leadership journey

Appointing leaders

When the board is looking for a new CEO, they are not just looking for a person with leadership qualities (however those may be defined): many people have leadership qualities. The board will be looking for a solution to whatever they think the major challenge is for their firm. This leads them to find someone who has already solved that problem before. For instance, the challenge for the firm may be about:

- going global
- restructuring and generating growth
- simplifying operations
- generating faster growth
- accelerating innovation and time to market

There are countless other challenges, and each one requires a very different skill set from the leader of the firm. It also means the leader and the firm will be engaged in very different sorts of activity. If the challenge is about going global, the leader will be spending more time on flights than if the challenge is to restructure domestic operations.

The same logic applies to appointing leaders at all levels: you look not just for the right person, but for the right solution. You need someone who will deliver the outcome you want. At more junior levels, the stakes are lower so you can take a risk and develop people in role. The more senior the appointment is, the higher the stakes become, and there will be lower risk appetite for taking a chance on someone without the right experience developing in role. This has major implications for how you develop your leadership career.

Managing your leadership journey

Increasingly, we cannot rely on employers for our careers. The median job tenure in the United States is now down to 4.1 years,[1] implying most people will change employers many times in their careers. Increasingly, career is becoming a verb, not a noun; we career from role to role, rather than having a career for life with a benevolent employer.

As a leader you need a portfolio of skills and experience. But you also need one or two claims to fame, where you are recognized as being best in class at doing something. In other words, you need both breadth and depth of experience.

If we have to manage our own leadership journey, it pays to have a map of where we are heading. Google may have mapped most things on our planet, but they have not yet produced a reliable leadership map, nor has anyone else. Table 8.1 shows a simplified map of a typical leadership journey.

TABLE 8.1 The leadership journey

Leadership level	Managing self: new employee	Managing others: front-line supervision	Managing a function: several teams	Managing a business with P&L	Managing a group of businesses
Time horizon	A day or a week	A week to a quarter	A quarter to a year	Over a year	Long-term future
Main task	Doing: quality, speed, craft skills, work planning	Managing: coach, motivate, performance manage, delegate	Optimizing: improve how things work	Integrating and changing	Leading
Who you value	Self	Your team	Other functions	Staff support	External stakeholders
Financial skills	N/A	Cost management	Budget management: negotiate and control	P&L management: revenue generation, cost allocation	Financial accounting: tax, reporting
Traps and challenges	Disenchantment: dull, boring work	Not changing your game	Not managing politics	From impostor syndrome to hubris	Losing touch

Source J Owen (2015) *Mindset of Success*, 2nd edn, Kogan Page, London

Here are a few of the main changes that happen on most leadership journeys, from emerging to senior leader:

- Time horizon goes from short term to long term. As a new graduate, you will be given tasks that need to be completed in a few hours or days. By the time you are the CEO, you will be planning years ahead.
- The key skills go from technical or craft skills to people and political skills. When you start your career, you will learn a craft such as accounting, law, teaching, or preparing PowerPoint presentations. By the time you reach the top, you will be getting other people to do these things for you.
- Financial skills become increasingly important over time. At the start of a career, most people have no budget other than their own time; at board level there is relentless focus on financial performance and presentation.
- Staff go from being the enemy who stop you doing things, to allies who help you make things happen.

Leaders who fail to learn and grow become marooned: they hit a career ceiling which they cannot break through. If you want to keep moving along your leadership journey, keep learning.

Lessons for leaders

There is a very simple message for leaders at all levels: keep on growing, keep on learning, keep on changing.

Build capabilities which you know will be in demand somewhere all the time: cutting costs, growing revenues and improving operations are capabilities which never go out of fashion. Even if your skill is not top of the agenda at your firm, it will be top of the agenda somewhere else. If you want to control your future, your employability is more important than your employer.

No matter where you are on your leadership journey, you will find that your context keeps on changing. That means you have to change as well. Three examples will make the point.

The emerging leader

Your first promotion is often the most hazardous step on your leadership journey. If a new graduate does a good job, promotion will ensue. The graduate will then naturally do more of the same: when you have a success model, stick to it. The graduate then gets fired, not because they have become incompetent but because they have not realized that the game has changed.

The new graduate is like the great footballer who is promoted to coach. The increased responsibility does not mean that the player has to play harder or better: the player has to learn a new role. The job of the coach is not to score all the goals, make all the tackles and play beautiful passes. The job of the coach is to select and develop the right team and to decide the right tactics. The same is true for the graduate: they no longer have to do all the work themselves, but they have to help the team do the work effectively. New leaders must make the crucial transition from asking 'How do I do this?' to 'Who can do this?' Moving from 'how' to 'who' changes everything.

The entrepreneurial leader

The classic entrepreneur always seems to start in a garage or a bedroom, or occasionally at the kitchen table. This is when you discover or develop new talents, because you have to be able to do everything. You are your own personal assistant, IT help desk, sales force, product development team, financial controller and bookkeeper. It can almost make you nostalgic for the days when you were enabled and imprisoned by the corporate life support systems of most large firms.

As you succeed, you can start to hire staff. This means you can focus your role where you make the most difference. Your context is changing, so you change. Your role continues to focus as the firm grows. But many entrepreneurs struggle with the change, because they do not want to give up direct control. They interfere where they should delegate, which demoralizes the team and overworks the leader. They become the classic overbearing entrepreneurial leader: 'My way or no way.' Success proves to them that they are right; failure proves to them that they cannot trust other people. Inevitably, the firm becomes highly dependent on them. This is not sustainable.

Even when you are the founder of the firm, you have to keep growing and adapting if you are to build a sustainable firm.

All leaders

Think of your favourite movies and music. What age were you when they were first produced? Many people believe that there was a golden era when they were in their late teens and early twenties: anything earlier is old fashioned, and anything since then is just not as good. We get stuck in our own cultural time warp. At a personal level, that is not a problem. At a professional level, it is a big problem. We have to cultivate a mindset which is open to new ideas, new experiences and to learning new things. If the best is always in the past, we cannot move forward.

Conclusion

Misunderstand what leaders do and you can find yourself appointing the wrong leader (end of firm) or acquiring the wrong experience (end of career). So this slightly dull and technical myth is very dangerous. Leadership is a journey, not a destination. This means you have to keep learning and growing because the rules of survival and success keep changing.

Note

1 Bureau of Labor Statistics. Employee tenure in 2020, news release, 2020, www.bls.gov/news.release/pdf/tenure.pdf (archived at https:// perma.cc/Q2S4-YUML)

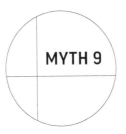

Leadership should be transformational: Charisma and an ability to inspire are key

The need for heroes runs deep.

Charisma and inspiration are part of the hero myth. Down the ages, people have looked to the great leader who will take them to the Promised Land. The great heroes of history live on in books and as statues in main squares. The really great ones have movies made about them. Each country is selective about its heroes and its heroic stories. The English remember Henry V defeating the French at Agincourt a mere 600 years ago, and Shakespeare wrote an eponymous play about it. But the English get very vague about how Joan of Arc beat the English in return, whereas the French celebrate her as a heroine.

The statues, history books and movies all reinforce the message that great people achieve great things. These heroes are always larger than life. Even if they were modest in their day, stories and mythology attach to them over time like barnacles to a ship.

The need for heroes runs deep. We want leaders who can transform our fortunes, or at least transform our working day so that we can do better. Our leaders may not be able to cast wizards' spells; instead they reach out for the latest miracle medicine being peddled by consultants and academics who claim to have found the solution to your strategy, operations, processes, leadership or teamworking. The desire for magic is still there and we keep on buying the medicine bottle, in a triumph of hope over reality.

The idea of a charismatic and inspirational leader is closely linked to the theory of transformational leadership (see Myth 3). Believing in this theory offers hope of a better future. It is an offer we all want to believe in, which makes us ready to believe the charismatic leader.

Why this myth matters

The transformational leader focuses on building trust within their team. They engage them and bring them to a higher level of motivation and purpose, creating a strong sense of identity and mission. They are charismatic and inspirational, with a high ability to motivate, influence and persuade. They challenge the status quo and seek change. The idea is that people will want to perform well and find purpose in reaching for a demanding vision. Individuals will be prepared to put the vision and team before themselves.

On one level, transformational leadership is a nice idea. It works well with professionals who push back against micro-management, but want to find meaning and purpose in their work. But as a theory, the expectations are too high. The way that leaders are expected to be in order to fit the notion of a transformational leader (a charismatic and inspirational hero) demands too much from them.

The idea that leaders need to be charismatic and inspirational is both dangerous and useful. It is dangerous because charisma and inspiration are largely unattainable and are not necessary:

- *Effective leaders are rarely charismatic*. Think of the leaders in your business, from team leaders to the big boss at the top. How many of them would you rate as charismatic and inspirational? I have interviewed thousands of leaders: many of them are exceptional, but very few were charismatic and inspirational. The most charismatic one is currently under investigation for fraud.

- *Charisma and inspiration are not always forces for good*. Like the Force in *Star Wars*, it has a dark side. Genghis Khan, Mao Tse-tung, Adolf Hitler, Mussolini and Pol Pot were all charismatic and inspirational in their own ways. Psychopaths are often charismatic: they are very good at reading people and manipulating them.

- *You cannot teach charisma and inspiration*. That means you are born with charisma or you are not, in which case we may as well select leaders at birth based on finding the charisma gene. So far, medical science has not invented the charisma transplant operation.

- *Charisma is not the solution*. Modern business is so complicated that it cannot rely on the inspiration of one person. Breakthrough ideas can come from anywhere, and implementation can be a huge team effort.

The myth is useful because it points to two requirements of leaders today. Charisma and inspiration are founded on the twin pillars of hope and motivation. Effective leaders have to offer hope, and they have to engage their team. Leaders need willing and motivated followers (see Myth 10).

Lessons for leaders

If charisma and inspiration are a dead end, what is the alternative? research shows that followers expect five things from their leaders.[1] Here they are, in order of priority:

Vision

Give your team a clear sense of purpose, direction and hope. This is not an abstract vision about improving shareholder returns, because your team may well not care about shareholder returns. It is a concrete vision which shows how each member of your team can make a difference, how their future will be better and how they are contributing to something worthwhile and meaningful.

Ability to motivate

Part of motivation is about structure: ensure each team member has a balanced set of tasks. Inevitably there will be some dull and routine work, but there should also be challenging and interesting work. Leaders motivate most by doing one thing: they show that they care about each team member and their future. That means taking an interest in them, giving them honest and constructive feed-back regularly, assigning them the right tasks, recognizing their contributions in public, and even saying 'thank you' once in a while.

Decisive

If you really want to demotivate and annoy your team, make decisions slowly and then keep on changing your mind. This will ensure that your team will endure the maximum of uncertainty and the maximum amount of rework. Teams crave clarity, so give it to them. Even if the situation is uncomfortable, clarity and decisiveness create a way forward and offer the hope of a solution.

Good in a crisis

A crisis is what separates a leader from the rest. It is the moment leaders take control and shine. Crisis manage-ment is about what you do and how you do it. What you do means looking forward, finding solutions and driving to action rather than analysing the past to find who to blame. Even more important is how you carry yourself. If you are positive, professional and constructive then you will leave the impression that you are in control and you know what you are doing (even if you have huge doubts yourself). If you run around like a headless chicken, then your panic will spread across your team.

Honest

The research asked about honesty, and it scored highly. Most of us want to work for an honest person but the evidence is that many people are also very happy to work for crooks, psychopaths and dictators. So the research dug into the honesty question and found that followers really want something even more powerful than honesty: they want trust. No one wants to work for a leader they do not trust. How you build trust is the subject of Myth 17.

Conclusion

As a leader you have to be transformational; this is essential if you want to make a difference. But the idea of the charismatic and inspirational leader is not only a myth, it is a dangerous myth. Charisma and inspiration are unattainable and unteachable for most of us, and are not necessary; leaders who have charisma can turn out to be dangerous demagogues and fraudsters.

If you can deliver on the five expectations above, you will be a highly effective leader and very professional. You will have a vision of hope and the ability to motivate which will make people want to follow you. You do not have to be charismatic to make a difference.

Note

1 Author's original research based on interviews with successful leaders, originally published in Jo Owen (2015) *How to Lead*, Pearson, London. Each of these leadership requirements is covered in detail in this book, with a separate myth for each one.

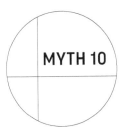

MYTH 10

Leaders communicate well and motivate their followers

There is a huge reality gap between the perceptions of leaders and their followers.

The link between motivation and communication is clear: if you can't communicate your message well, it's unlikely that people will feel motivated to follow you. The good news is that 67 per cent of leaders think that they are good at motivation. The bad news is that only 32 per cent of their followers agree.[1] There is a huge reality gap between the perceptions of leaders and their followers. You may think you are good at motivation, but what does your team really think?

Adding motivation to the long list of job requirements of a leaders is daunting. It is also unhelpful. You cannot tell people to be motivated, happy or positive. These things come from within. All a leader can do is to create the conditions where people discover their intrinsic motivation, and to stop doing things which demotivate the team. That is more achievable and practical than demanding that leaders be motivational.

Leaders can also think about how they communicate, and whether this serves to motivate or demotivate their team. Some leaders go down in history as great communicators: Churchill, Martin Luther King and even Ronald Reagan. In the meantime, we have to put up with PowerPoint presentations which are death by bullet point. We suffer tedious meetings and endless urgent emails at all times of day and night copied to everyone on a just-in-case basis. This does nothing for motivation. We can talk to people halfway round the world, but still our intentions get lost in translation. Technology has enabled an explosion of communication which would astound our ancestors. But although we communicate more than ever, we understand each other as little as ever. For leaders, the answer is often to think about how much they are communicating and the medium they are using to do it in order to provide the conditions for their team to discover their intrinsic motivation.

Why this myth matters

The nature of leadership has changed. In the past, leaders expected compliance from their teams. They had the power and authority to enforce compliance. Given that most work was routine and easy to measure, compliance was enough. But the nature of work has changed, which has forced leaders to change how they lead. Work is now much more ambiguous: what does a 'good' report or meeting look like? How much time and effort should go into each piece of work? Professional work is, by its nature, ambiguous. The growth of the professions means their productivity is more important. But how do you measure the output of a consultant, psychotherapist or health and safety officer? It is not like measuring quantity and quality on a production line.

In this new world of work, compliance is not enough. You need real commitment from the team to deliver quality which is more than 'good enough'. Time and cost pressures mean that there is a real squeeze, so leaders rely on their team to keep on going the extra mile to make things happen.

Added to this, technology has changed how we communicate. Technology allows us to communicate more than ever. But quality does not always increase with quantity. It is easy to drown in a tidal wave of emails, instant messages and back-to-back video calls. This matters for three reasons:

1 The signal is lost in the noise: what matters is submerged by trivia.
2 24/7 communication means leaders can never switch off: they then burn out, stress out and drop out.
3 Technology is great for transactions, lousy for trust. Building relationships is far easier in person than remotely. The first person to work out how to motivate by email will make a fortune. It is a fortune which is unlikely to be made.

Lessons for leaders

Emerging research and practice[2] shows that leaders can do four things to help people rediscover their intrinsic motivation, summarized as the RAMP principle:

supportive **R**elationships
Autonomy
Mastery
Purpose

In more detail:

- *Supportive relationships*: This moves the leader from being a boss to a coach who develops each team member. That may include having difficult, but supportive, conversations about improving performance. It means protecting them.
- *Autonomy*: Professionals do not like being micro-managed, so manage them less. Delegate more and let them over-achieve for you. The rise of hybrid working and working from home means that professionals have tasted autonomy and now want it more than ever. Give it to them.
- *Mastery*: It is hard to be motivated if you lack the skills for today's role and you are not building skills for the future. As a leader, stretch your team and help them grow; coach them and do not solve every problem for them.
- *Purpose*: A compelling vision is highly motivational. Throughout history, people have made extraordinary sacrifices for their visions of peace, power, freedom and

religion. You can craft a meaningful vision by telling a simple story (see Myth 12) and communicating it well:

○ This is where we are.
○ This is where we are going.
○ This is how we will get there (and this is your vital role in helping us get there).

Hone your communication skills to get the most out of your team. Leaders have to tame the communications beast. That means:

- Discover the 'off' switch. Have times of night (and day) when it is OK to sleep and not reply to the next urgent email.
- Listen more, talk less. All the best leaders and sales people have two ears and one mouth, and use them in that proportion. Listening is your secret weapon of building relationships, trust and influence, and gaining knowledge.
- Choose the right medium. Use technology for transactions and routine matters. Use face to face for difficult conversations, influencing and persuading people and motivating your team.
- Focus on the signal, avoid the noise. Keep focused on your big message and avoid too much detail. Focus on the right person: kill 'copy all' which is a good way of generating noise and unnecessary work as everyone chips in with their thoughts.
- Stay positive. People will remember the messenger long after they have forgotten the message. They will remember if you were positive, supportive and action focused or if you were negative, undermining and passive. Choose well.

Finally, there is one statement which is an unerringly reliable predictor of whether your followers will think that you are a good and motivational boss or not:

My boss cares for me and my career. (Agree/Disagree)

Followers who thought their boss cared for them and their career rated their boss positively on nearly all other criteria; bosses who scored low on this question scored low on everything else. Showing you really care takes time and effort: it is an investment of time which pays rich dividends.

Conclusion

Leaders should communicate well to motivate their followers, so that is not a myth. But in reality, many leaders are not good communicators or motivators, and that inhibits their ability to lead. The myth exists in practice, if not in theory.

Notes

1 Author's original research with over 500 leaders and followers, first published in J Owen (2015) *How to Lead*, Pearson, London
2 See the work of STIR education on building intrinsic motivation for millions of teachers, officials and children across India and Africa. The author is founding chair of STIR.

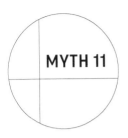

MYTH 11

Leaders are brave and decisive

*You cannot know the answer if you
do not know the question.*

There are two myths here which have common roots:

1 Leaders are brave.
2 Leaders are decisive.

Bravery and decisiveness are part of the largely discredited Great Man theory of leadership (see Myth 3). Only the Great Man can be trusted to make the right decisions, and only they are brave enough to do it.

The brave and decisive leader conjures up images of generals on horseback issuing orders and leading their army to victory: you never see paintings of the losing general fleeing on horseback. Despite the Great Man theory of leadership being largely discredited, both leaders and followers happily subscribe to these myths, with adverse results. I'll unpack them in turn.

Leaders are brave

We need leaders to be courageous – research shows that it's as important as ever. However, the nature of courage has changed.[1] Courage is consistently identified as one of the seven mindsets which separate the best leaders from the rest. This makes sense. If a leader takes people where they would not have got by themselves, then that involves taking risk. And taking any sort of risk requires courage because risks can lead to failure. That means you can only lead if you are brave.

Why this myth matters

Courage stands at the heart of what modern leaders have to do:

- *Make decisions.* Even in organizations with the most long-winded decision-making processes, someone ultimately needs to make the final call.
- *Have difficult conversations.* Problems such as under-performance and unrealistic expectations about promotions and pay need to be tackled head-on. Waiting for a year-end review can erode trust because you will have failed to deal with the truth early.
- *Take risks.* No one gets fired for missing an opportunity; many get fired for taking a risk and missing. Good

leaders step up and take the risk. The sorts of risks that leaders have to take are personal and emotional. Success has many friends, but failure is very lonely. When risk goes sour, the consequences can be embarrassing or career limiting.

Lessons for leaders

At first, it would appear that there are no lessons for leaders: you are either brave or you are not brave. You can't learn to be brave, can you?

The Fire Brigade shows that you can teach bravery. They help raw recruits to do brave things in easy steps. They start by teaching them about their kit. Then they teach them how to extinguish a fire in a chip pan. They continue by teaching them how to deal with progressively frightening situations. Eventually, they are doing things that you or I would think are crazy brave.

Leaders, like firemen, can acquire bravery in small steps. Learn to take small risks: don't make your first public speech in front of 2,000 key managers at your firm's global conference. Start with a small talk to a small group of trusted colleagues on a familiar topic. Work up from there.

As with firemen, much of what appears to be bravery is simply pattern recognition; once you have seen a situation enough times, you know what to expect and you will have the confidence to deal with it.

The Royal Marines Commandos teach us one more lesson about bravery. Bravery is relative to your context. The commandos may, at some point, literally risk their lives. That is extreme bravery, which takes more than training. It takes indoctrination of core values, which are reinforced through rewards, sanctions, teamwork, culture and stories. At the opposite extreme is the classic machine bureaucracy where changing the coffee machine might be seen as a bold move. Inevitably, both extremes will recruit candidates with the basic aptitudes they require, including a higher or lower appetite for risk and adventure.

As a leader, you do not need to put your life on the line. You do not need to be as brave as a commando or a fireman; you just need to be braver than your peers.

If you want to cultivate the bravery of a leader, your keys to success are:

- *Take small steps*. Take small risks first and work up from there.
- *Gain experience*. Keep putting yourself in situations where you can learn patterns of success and failure. This will give you the confidence to deal with such situations in future.
- *Be relatively brave*. You only need to be braver than your peers, and braver than you were last year. You do not need to put your life or your career on the line every day.

Leaders are decisive

In just the same way that we want leaders to be brave, we also want them to be decisive. One of the top five expectations that followers have of their leaders is decisiveness. The alternative is a nightmare. Indecisive leaders mean that the team has to spend half its time trying to guess what the leader will do, and the rest of the time re-working things after the leader has changed his or her mind. Decisiveness creates clarity and focus and gives the team what they want.

Decisiveness is better than indecision. End of story. But is it end of story?

Why this myth matters

Leaders often like to be the general on horseback. The person the leader trusts most on their team is themselves, so they are often comfortable making the big decisions. Teams are also more than happy to delegate upwards. When things go wrong, it absolves them of all responsibility. Seen in this light, decisiveness is more of a vice than a virtue because it shows:

- the leader lacks trust in the team and is not prepared to delegate decision making
- the team wants to avoid responsibility by delegating decision making upwards

There is an alternative. In Japan, leaders will often issue quite vague and apparently contradictory directions such as 'we need to increase profitability and we need to increase market share'. Sometimes this is because the manager is weak and does not know what to do, but often it is a deliberate decision by a good leader. They know that in a hierarchical society like Japan, if they give instructions then the team will follow them literally: the team will have no discretion. So the best way to find the best solution is not to give specific instructions, but to give broad priorities. That leaves the team free to find the best solution.

The great leader does not need a white horse, and does not need to make all the decisions.

Lessons for leaders

Leaders have to be able to make decisions: you cannot avoid it. The decisions which really matter are often high risk and have high uncertainty. That is why most organizations are addicted to committees and long decision-making processes. If everyone is implicated in making the wrong decision, then there is no one to blame. But that is followership, not leadership.

The trap for leaders is to regard decision making as an intellectual exercise to which there is a right or wrong solution. That may have been true at school where you were set clear exam questions. In business, often the greatest challenge is to find out what question you need to ask, and what questions you can ignore. You cannot know the answer if you do not know the question.

Even when you have found the right exam question, the solution is not just an intellectual exercise. Organizations are full of people, and that makes them political. Good decision making is both logical and political.

The only good decision is one which leads to action. In the old world of command and control, that meant issuing orders. In today's world that means there has to be fair process around decision making. The decision must engage people so that they accept, own and will act on the decision. The lessons for leaders are about the logical and political aspects of making decisions.

LOGICAL DECISION MAKING IN UNCERTAINTY

The intellectual principles for making a decision are:

- *Recognize the pattern.* Business sense is simply pattern recognition. Back yourself. If you do not recognize the pattern, find someone who does and consult them.
- *Follow the strategy and the values.* At moments of uncertainty and ambiguity, with limited data, how do you choose? This is where a clear strategy and strong sense of values will guide you in the right direction. The strategy and values may not tell you what to do, but they can tell you what not to do. That is valuable.
- *What does the data say?* Evidence-based decision making is better than guesswork and should be used to weigh up the pros and cons of each path of action. But for many leaders, evidence-based decision making is code for 'find me the evidence to support my decision'. Leaders often use data like drunks use lamp posts: for support, not illumination.
- *Who does this decision matter to?* Look at the decision through the eyes of different stakeholders and understand what options will not work and will be highly resisted. Identify the solutions which are most likely to gain support. You do not want an intellectually brilliant decision which dies on first contact with political reality.
- *Drive to action.* Formal decision-making tools like Bayesian analysis, or perhaps mind maps, fishbones or SWOT analyses can help but can also be excuses for inaction: 'analysis paralysis'. The problem with analysis is that there is always another fact to be found, another

analysis to be run. The perfect solution does not exist in an imperfect and changing world: the perfect is the enemy of the good. At some point, you have to make your mind up.

POLITICAL DECISION MAKING: FAIR PROCESS

An effective decision is one which leads to action. That requires fair process in how you make the decision. You have to involve your team and other stakeholders appropriately. If you can delegate the decision, delegate it. Like the Japanese, you can set the broad priorities and let the team decide on how best to get there. By doing this you are not just delegating the decision. You are also delegating the responsibility and ownership for the decision. The result is that you will have a team which is committed to making the idea work. People rarely argue with their own idea, so let the idea be theirs.

If you cannot delegate the decision, then fair process remains important. You can at least consult your team and others before making the decision. This is a process the Japanese called *nemawashi*: building agreement in private one by one. In private, all the influencers and stakeholders can say what they really think, and you can align all their agendas and gain their tacit support. The subsequent meeting is not to make the decision, but to confirm in public the agreement that has been reached in private: it is a commitment process, not just a decision process. This process is highly political: welcome to the real world.

When communicating the decision, fair process requires more than just the decision. For the team to understand the decision properly, they need the full context: why the decision was made, what the alternatives were, and the pros and cons involved. It is not enough to communicate the decision, you have to sell it.

Conclusion

These myths are both true. Leaders do need to be brave and decisive. But the nature of bravery has changed since the days of history and the nature of leadership bravery is widely misunderstood. In addition, leaders who are too decisive are control freaks, which is not leadership. Making decisions in uncertainty and making them stick in an organization is very tough and rarely done well.

Note

1   J Owen (2015) *Mindset of Success*, Kogan Page, London

MYTH 12

Leaders are visionary

Leaders are peddlers of hope.

Research shows that the most important thing followers expect from their leader is a clear vision.[1] And when we think of all the great leaders, they all have great visions. Kennedy sent men to the Moon for the first time; Martin Luther King gave his famous 'I have a dream' speech. So it seems to be case closed: leaders need to be visionary.

But we should pause before we walk away, for two reasons:

- First, grand visions are dangerous. Every mad dictator down the ages has had a crazed vision. Some want to conquer the world, others want to conquer the enemy within. These are visions which have led to millions of deaths. For every visionary who marches you to the Promised Land, there is another who marches you straight back into the desert and to death.

· Second, if you are leading a team it is hard to have a grand vision. If you feel the urge one Monday morning to stand on your desk and announce to your team, 'I have a dream...' your team may wonder what you put in your coffee.

Visions are problematic for normal leaders. The greater the visions, the more dangerous and less credible they become to your team. But what is the point of a small vision?

Why this myth matters

Having a vision matters for all leaders. Leaders take people where they would not have got by themselves. If you don't know where you are going, then you will not get there and your team will be confused at best. Without a vision, you cannot lead.

This means we have to understand what a vision really means for leaders. For a team and its leader, an effective vision has three parts:

· an idea
· a promise of hope
· a call to action

These three elements allow you to craft a compelling vision which is relevant and credible to your situation.

Lessons for leaders

Here is how you can build your vision based on the three elements.

An idea

It is hard to have a vision, but we can all have ideas. A visionary idea is no more than a story in three parts, as follows:

- This is where we are.
- This is where we are going.
- This is how we will get there.

We can all tell a story, and that is all we need to do. We can dress it up as a strategic initiative if that makes people feel better about it. But at the heart of any strategy, vision or idea is a simple story which you can tell about how you will make a difference.

Big ideas beat small ideas, because they excite and energize people more. If you have an idea about rationalizing the use of paper clips in your office, that is worthy but you will not get many people excited about it. Big ideas are noticed across the organization; they are ideas where you make a difference. They will attract both support and opposition. Dare to be bold.

A promise of hope

Leaders are peddlers of hope. Cynical and junior team members tend to stay that way: cynical and junior. No leader succeeds by peddling gloom. Even in Britain's darkest hour, when defeat to the Nazis looked likely, Churchill peddled hope, not gloom. He reached his rhetorical heights: 'Never in the field of human history has so much been owed by so many to so few... this was their finest hour... we will fight them on the beaches...'. He did not resort to the middle management blame game: 'I warned you in my email that this would happen.'

Every vision must have a promise of hope. Your idea has to show how things will be better in the future, both for the firm and for the individual. This makes your vision far more than a plan or a budget. Meeting a budget is not a promise of hope: it is a requirement to be met. Your idea has to show how things will be different and better in the future.

A call to action

Your vision may be important to you, but that does not mean it is important to anyone else. If your idea is to transform the supply chain, that could be very good for the business, but your team may not be impressed. Some will think that it has nothing to do with them; they will shrug their shoulders and focus on what they need to buy for dinner that evening. Others may wonder if your vision means that they will lose their job; are you going to march them to the Promised Land or to the desert? Do not expect your team to fall in love with an abstract idea.

To make your vision meaningful, you have to make it personal to each team member. You have to answer the two questions each team member will have:

- *How will this affect me?* New ideas provoke both fear and hope. Fears are natural: will this mean more work, will I have to learn new skills, will this affect my pay and promotion prospects? Show how your idea will help your team members grow and develop.

- *What is my role?* If you can paint a picture which shows that each team member has a vital role in helping the vision become reality, then you increase their commitment. Giving your team members a sense of control, involvement, relevance and purpose is highly motivational.

Your vision will mean different things to different people. Each person will be asking the WIFM question: 'What's In It For Me?' Help them answer that positively. Remember that visions are not just about ideas: they are about people.

Conclusion

Leaders do not need to be visionary like Martin Luther King, but they do need to have a vision or idea of what they will achieve. Being visionary is about style; having a vision is about substance.

Note

1   Author's original research with over 500 leaders and followers, first published in J Owen (2015) *How to Lead*, Pearson, London

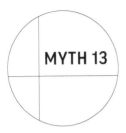

MYTH 13

Leaders set goals and give directions

Clear goals are of no use unless they are shared goals.

This myth is, in fact, a truism. All leaders set goals and give directions: if they don't set goals and give directions they have no chance of taking people where they would not have got by themselves.

Case closed.

Pause for a moment before you file this case away in your number one file, the waste basket. What makes sense at first does not always make sense on closer inspection. This is a regular discovery for anyone who has a bright idea in the bar one evening, and wakes up the next morning to discover that their idea is not quite as bright as the dawn.

This apparent truism contains two fatal flaws.

The minor problem is that it does not differentiate between leaders and managers. Both leaders and managers need to set goals and give directions. Teachers set goals and give directions. Supervisors set goals and give directions. Sports coaches set goals and give directions. Teachers, supervisors and coaches may be supremely professional and good at their tasks, but that does not necessarily make them leaders. So setting goals and giving directions is part of leadership, but it does not define leadership. It is like breathing: necessary but not sufficient to lead, and it fails to separate leaders from the rest.

The major problem is that leaders are not very good at setting goals and giving directions. Research on the effectiveness of global teams found that they face big challenges around trust, communications and culture. But 65 per cent of team members said goal setting was a problem.[1] This was a surprising finding. Setting goals is Management 101: how on earth could high-flying, globetrotting leaders be so poor at goal setting?

As with many of the myths of leadership, the practice of leadership often struggles to keep up with the theory. This does not show that leaders are fools: it shows that leadership is exceptionally hard. Even getting the basics right is hard. This is true, not just for leaders, but for top sports people and musicians. We can all kick a football, but try controlling and kicking it in the right direction when moving at high speed and under huge pressure from the opposition. What looks simple can be very hard, and this is true of goal setting.

Why this myth matters

If leaders struggle to set goals and give directions well, then they struggle to lead. Doing this well is fundamental to your success as a leader.

Lessons for leaders

Process matters

Leaders often make the mistake of thinking that goal setting is about clear goals. That is only half the story. Clear goals are of no use unless they are also shared goals. Your team has to own the goals. Leaders will spend a huge amount of time thinking about their goals and how to frame them, because it is genuinely difficult to fix the right goals. Too often, they then expect their team or firm to internalize months of thinking as a result of a brilliant 40-minute speech. That is never going to happen.

If you want your team to own your goals, you have to take them on your journey. The best way to do that is to involve them from the start. If your team believes that the goals are their idea, they will be committed to them: people do not argue against their own ideas. If they have been involved from the start, they will understand the context, the thinking and the trade-offs. They will understand how to act in ambiguous situations.

Involving the team from the start is ideal but not always practical. It means you will have to invest heavily in selling and explaining your idea after the event. After a two-year turnaround, one CEO remarked: 'Figuring out what to do was easy. That took 5 per cent of my time. Thirty-five per cent of my time was spent working on the plan. Sixty per cent of my time was spent selling it and then selling it again. I could not believe it took so long.' Taking people where they would not have got by themselves means you have to persuade them and keep on persuading them.

Context matters

When talking about goals, leaders often focus on the what, who, when and where questions. They will then explore the 'how' question at length as required. The one question which is easy to forget but is the most important is 'why'. Your team wants to know not just the goal, but the context for the goal: why did you pick this goal and what were the other options? What are the trade-offs and how should they be handled? They will only understand the context properly if you have managed the process of goal setting properly.

Manage the trade-offs

The two best moments of owning a boat are the day you buy it and the day you sell it. The same is true of goal setting: the two best days are the day you set the goal and the day you achieve the goal. The time in between is a struggle. The day you set the goal you have clarity and hope. The next day, reality sets in. You face three challenges:

1 *Sacrifice*. If you ask for one thing, others tend to slip. Focus on profits and customer service slips; focus on efficiency and you lose flexibility; reduce risks and

innovation is reduced. There is no free lunch. Bold leaders are ready to make these sacrifices. Weaker leaders go for the balanced scorecard approach which ensures that they get a little of everything: that is good management but not good leadership.

2 *Game playing.* The good news is that everyone will want to achieve the goals you set. The bad news is that they will play games to get there. Cheating doesn't just happen in sports with drug taking and professional fouls; it happens in every walk of life. In education, governments keep on setting new goals, and even trustworthy teachers cheat the system. For instance, what is wrong with requiring that all 16-year-olds show they are numerate and literate? Here is how a school could react:

- *By narrowing the curriculum to focus on literacy and numeracy.* Out go important things like becoming employable, sports, music and drama; and all the other academic subjects get squeezed as well.
- *By focusing all efforts on children on the pass/fail margin.* Ignore the high achievers because they can look after themselves; ignore the low performers because they will fail anyway.
- *By teaching to test.* Focus on drilling students on how to answer the exam questions, which is separate from helping them to become literate or numerate. The dull drills put children off education for life.

All of this can help the school to look good in exam results, but at the cost of not giving the students a good education. Game playing is normal: manage it.

3 *Competition and teamwork*. There is real tension between collective and individual goals. This cuts to the heart of how far your team is a team or just a group of individuals with separate goals; it also cuts to the heart of the accountability and collaboration challenge. Collective goals are good for collaboration, but weak on individual accountability. Individual goals encourage each person to retreat into their own silo and you lose cooperation. There is no magic answer. Recognize that your leadership team is only a team for some challenges, and is a group of individuals for others. Know which is which and set goals accordingly.

Conclusion

This problem appears repeatedly: the theory is a truism, but the practice of leadership does not live up to the theory.

Note

1 J Owen (2016) *Global Teams*, FT Publishing, 121–42

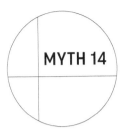

Great leaders build great teams

Teams, like firms, constantly slide towards the chaos of entropy.

This is another modern myth which is set against the Great Man theory of leadership. Its main ally in the fight against the Great Man theory is the theory of distributed leadership, in which leadership is shared among a group, rather than relying on one person. It is a way of engaging the whole team effectively and optimizing performance. (These theories were introduced in Myth 3). If leadership is no longer about the lone hero, then by default you need to have a great team to achieve great things.

Why this myth matters

Unless you happen to be a great man or woman, you will need a great team to achieve great things. Your power lies in the power of your organization, not just in your personal power and brilliance. This is a cruel lesson which many senior executives discover too late in their careers. As they progress through their firm, they get used to the trappings of power. Doors open for them, both literally and figuratively. They have easy access to decision makers. Hubris is when you believe that you can only turn left at the aircraft door.

And then the time comes for the senior executive to move aside for a younger generation. Suddenly, they find that doors no longer open for them either figuratively or literally, and that you can turn right at the aircraft doors without dying. Decision makers no longer return your calls, and you have no one to chase up for you. A horrible discovery looms: no one wanted to talk to you because of who you were, but because of who you represented. This is when the value of the team and the firm comes home: any leader is only as good as the followers they have. If you have no followers, you are not leading and you have no power.

Lessons for leaders

In theory, great leaders need great teams. In practice, leaders often struggle to build the team that will fulfil their ambitions. Distributed leadership touches on two vital aspects of leadership: control and delegation. To build a great team, you need to be able to delegate but the more you do this the more you face the challenge of control. Building the trust to delegate is partly about building personal trust in each member of your team. Finding a smart way to ensure control will make you more confident to delegate and build the great team you need.

Build control mechanisms

- *Recruit to values, not just to skills.* Research consistently shows that values and attitudes are better predictors of performance than raw skills.[1] For instance, Met Life decided to test its life assurance sales recruits for skills and optimism. As a test, it decided to take on candidates who had just failed the skills test but scored high on optimism: the unskilled optimists outsold the skilled recruits by an average of 70 per cent. You can teach skills, but not optimism or values. Your team also needs skills. But skills without values is a recipe for disaster. To delegate with confidence, you need to know your team members have not only the right skills but the right values too. To build trust, team members can be of any race, faith or gender but they have to adhere to the idea of the 'one firm firm'. Diversity of values is not tolerated. As one leader put it: 'I find I always hire for skills and fire for values.'
- *Ensure you have the right information and processes.* The explosion of data available to leaders today means that it is possible to have more information faster than ever before. Information and trust are usually inversely proportional: high levels of reporting reflect low levels of trust. Very high levels of information allow the leader to micro-manage. They should also allow the leader to delegate more: you

can be confident that the data will show you when you need to step back in. Process control is equally important. Walter Lingle is an unsung hero of globalization. He globalized Procter & Gamble and its brand management system with a simple insight: if all the successful processes and procedures of Cincinnati HQ could be replicated down to specifying the length and format of the monthly brand report, then you could let each country manage its own brands successfully. Control was vested in the system, backed up by a few international executives who ensured the systems were being applied correctly.

Shake up the legacy team

It is common for new leaders to shake up their teams. There are three reasons you may want to do this:

- *To take control.* Reorganizing is often a political as much as a rational act. It is a way of removing power barons and blockers, and putting in people you trust and can depend on. It sends a signal that you are ready to take control through delegation. You're happy to move people around and make difficult decisions.
- *To upgrade performance.* The legacy team may well have found its comfort zone, enabling it to perform well without breaking sweat.
- *To set a new direction.* The legacy team was there to address a legacy challenge: your predecessor's legacy. If you are to lead people where they would not have got by themselves you need a new and clear agenda. A new agenda means you probably need new skills and a new balance in the composition of your team.

The alternative is to live with the legacy team. The longer you live with it, the more you will be acquiescing in the old agenda, the old team and the old ways of working. It becomes harder to justify reorganizing the longer you leave the legacy team in place. Moving fast helps.

Keep on refreshing your team

Teams, like firms, constantly slide towards the chaos of entropy. Team members leave for good or poor reasons: to pursue their ambitions elsewhere, to make more money, because of illness, incompetence or stress, or for better work–life balance. The natural churn of your team is mirrored by the churn of events. Stuff happens. Yesterday's challenge and priorities will not be the same as tomorrow's. External pressures of technology, competition, customers and regulation force change as well as the never-ending internal pressures of new initiatives which have to be dealt with. Teams, like milk, can go off fast. Keep your team fresh.

Leaders value loyalty over competence

Most leaders have this blind spot. As one put it: 'Most sins are forgivable, but disloyalty is not one of them.' She was speaking the truth. Contrary to the popular image of bosses, most bosses are forgiving and for good reason: replacing team members takes time and effort and is risky. There is no guarantee that the replacement will be any better. Loyal team members are the last to be fired, although if you have a gold medal in incompetence then nothing will save you. This is useful knowledge when you are following: overt loyalty never does you any harm, while failing to support your boss fully at critical moments is a career limiting move. As a leader, you need to balance your desire for loyalty and continuity with your need for performance.

RECRUITING TO VALUES: THE SHOE REPAIR SHOPS

Timpson is a large chain of shoe repair shops in the UK. Repairing shoes is not glamorous. The stores tend to be pocket sized and wages are modest. And yet these workers have huge responsibility: they run the entire shop and have to be able to repair shoes, inscribe trophies and do all the chores of any small business. So how do you find the right people to make this business a success?

Initially, Timpson hired cobblers. If you want to repair shoes, then you need cobblers to repair shoes. What could possibly go wrong?

Everything can go wrong. Cobblers do not always have great customer management or business management skills, and these shops are all about managing customers and managing a business. But to find anyone who has all the required skills is impossible, unless you pay uneconomic salaries.

Timpson realized that you can train skills but you cannot train values, so they started to recruit to values. To make the point, they replaced the normal assessment forms with one page of Mr Men cartoons. On one side it had 'good' Mr Men like Mr Honest, Mr Keen and Mr Helpful. On the other side it had Mr Men from the Dark Side: Mr Fib, Mr Idle, Mr Grumpy. Store managers had to circle which Mr Man each candidate was most like. Candidates from the Dark Side were turned down, however much skill they had. The system worked well. It worked even better when they introduced some female alternatives.

Conclusion

The need for distributed leadership has been around for thousands of years. It is a reality of leadership which many leaders struggle with. It is true in theory that great leaders build great teams, but it is rarely true in practice. Most leaders could do better in building the dream team.

Note

1   M Seligman (1998) *Learned Optimism*, Pocket Books, New York. This research has been replicated in other industries and geographies.

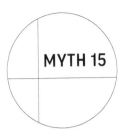

MYTH 15

The leader is in control and knows what is going on

The information you get is about the past.
The information you need is about the future.

If you don't know where you are, you are unlikely to know where you are going. Leaders have to know what is going on. And no leader will ever say that they are not in control: if you're not in control, you're not leading. But they can never be in full control of a large organization. It's impossible to know everything that is going on.

Leaders, like governments and businesses, have an insatiable appetite for knowing more and more. Dictators down the years have resorted to all sorts of ruses to know who is doing what, and where real or imagined treachery might lie. Today, we give away more information about what we do and what we think than any dictator of the past could have dreamed of finding. Businesses may know more about us than our loved ones know.

In the age of hyper information, leaders should be able to know exactly what is going on. In practice, the information leaders have and the information they want is not the same. Information is about the past, but leaders need to know about the future. Failing that, they need information which can guide them to their perfect future. But driving to the future by looking in the rear-view mirror is a recipe for disaster.

Why this myth matters

Unlike a deity, most leaders are not omnipresent, omniscient and omnipotent. The leaders who think they have these powers are well worth not working for. It is impossible to know in real time what is happening everywhere, let alone to do anything about it.

Organizations generate huge amounts of information: meetings, reports, emails and reviews can absorb all of the leader's time. But this huge amount of activity doesn't necessarily help achieve future goals.

The old saying is that 'knowledge is power'. The current equivalent is 'information is control'. Given that leaders are meant to be in control, they want information. And if more control is better, then that implies more information. Or, to put it the other way around, more information allows leaders to be in more control, so clearly more information is always more desirable. But is it?

Think of it in terms of business noise and your signal. Activity isn't the same as achievement. Noises are the daily distractions of business life; your signal is where you are going to make a difference. Effective leaders maximize their signal to noise ratio.

There is also the issue of trust. Trust is inversely proportional to control and information. The more information we demand and the more control we exert, the less trust we show in our teams. This is a dilemma for leaders. More professional and educated staff expect to be trusted more. But the deluge of hyper information is a temptation which few leaders can resist.

The challenge for leaders is to cut through the noise and know what information they really need, and what can be left to the organizational machine. How far can they avoid micro-managing through micro-information?

Lessons for leaders

Separate information from intelligence

The information you get is about the past. The information you need is about the future. We all wish we knew the future: that would be a short cut to making a fortune at the bookies.

Since you cannot know the future, however, you need an alternative which does not involve reading tea leaves and throwing chicken bones. As a leader, you will have a few projects which will help you shape and change the future. These are the projects where you need good information, which leads to rapid action.

The best way to start your information and reporting system is with a blank piece of paper. Write down what you really want to know, under the headings of budgets, people, customers/markets and projects. Then start to fill it in. The chances are that most of what you currently receive is not relevant and about half of what you do want is unavailable. But at least you have converted the unknown unknowns into known unknowns.[1]

To gather the intelligence, you need a balance between formal and informal information systems. Most leaders have limited trust in formal reports where evidence is used to support a position, not to illuminate the truth. Get out and meet customers, meet people on the front line and form your own opinion of reality. But do not be blinded by what you see: balance what your eyes see and what your information systems tell you. Neither is perfect, but together they give you a better chance of controlling what matters and shaping the future successfully.

Have a clear vision and focus on priorities: Maximize your signal

An old-fashioned watch has three hands: the hour hand, the minute hand and the second hand. Front-line staff watch the second hand: they are dealing with the here and now. Managers watch the second hand and the minute hand. The minute hand is about all the near-term goals and initiatives which they have to plan and execute. The leader watches all three hands. The hour hand is about the longer-term direction of the team and the firm.

As a leader, you need information about all three hands: if the second hand is not moving smoothly, then neither of the other hands can move. Most corporate reporting systems focus on the second hand, but although this generates huge amounts of data, not much is of use. It is useful mainly to manage risk: it shows what is not working and allows you to intervene on an exception basis. But it can suck you in: one piece of data generates demand for another to explain it. There is no escape from the noise.

To avoid getting sucked in, have a clear idea, or vision, of how things will be different or better as a result of your leadership. What will happen that would not have happened without you? This will help you to maximize your signal and focus on your priorities. You only need to intervene when the data shows that things are going materially off track, or are at risk of doing so. Materiality is key: if it is not material, delegate the challenge down and trust your team to deal with it. Your priorities might be as simple as:

- We will put our customers first.
- We will simplify our operations.
- We will be first to market.
- We will achieve Six Sigma quality.

At first blush, these appear to be no more than slogans. And if all you do is make the motivational speech about customers, it will remain a slogan. You then have to push the idea through to its logical conclusion. If customers come first, then that might mean making our products easy to use, making the helpline helpful, being generous on refunds, listening to what customers actually want, and much more.

The more you step back from micro-information management, the more trust you show in your team. It also allows you to focus your time on building your future.

Manage the noise: Build your team and organizational machine

To deal with the noise, the leader needs to put things in place: a great team and a strong organizational machine. Your team is your most vital asset: they can deliver the signal and manage the noise for you, and you only need to engage with the noise on an exception basis. But your team needs a machine that works. The plumbing of the firm is vital: decision-making systems, financial controls, reporting processes, operating systems, IT and people development systems all need to work. Plumbing may not be glamorous but it is essential: we only discover the true value of plumbing when it goes wrong.

Respect different perspectives

As a leader you may see the world from the top of the mountain, which allows you to see into the far distance. But never forget what it was like at the bottom of the mountain: in the farmyard you could see the chickens running around and the children playing in the street. These things are invisible from the top of the mountain. Your reporting system may tell you how many chickens and children there are, but it will not tell you what it is really like down in the farmyard.

You have to bridge the gap between the top and the bottom of the mountain. Climb down the mountain to find out what is really going on, and speak to people. You will discover what reporting systems can never tell you: what people think; what they see as the challenges and opportunities; and what are the obstacles they face in making your agenda work.

In the past, middle management were your Sherpa guides: they conveyed your orders to the bottom of the mountain and passed information about what was happening at the bottom back up to you. This meant that top management were often remote: they were stuck on the executive floor, with their executive dining room, toilets and parking spaces. To be effective, you need to be your own Sherpa. That means not only seeing life at the front line yourself, but also explaining the view from the top. The people in the farmyard cannot see your view and you need to explain what you see and how it affects them. Your vision is meaningless without context, and you are the best person to share that context.

Conclusion

Leaders can never know all that is going on, and above all they can never know the future. But the availability of information provides an irresistible temptation to meddle, micro-manage and demand even more information. This myth drives leaders to behave in the wrong way.

Note

1 'There are known knowns' is a phrase from a response given by former US Secretary of Defense Donald Rumsfeld to a question at a US Department of Defense news briefing on 12 February 2002 about the lack of evidence linking the government of Iraq with the supply of weapons of mass destruction to terrorist groups.

Leaders are born, not bred

If we do believe that leaders are born, not bred,
then most people may as well give up.

The nature versus nurture debate has been going on for decades, and possibly for millennia. Research shows that if you come from the right social background you are far more likely to succeed: this is less about talent and more about having an advantageous upbringing, socially and educationally. Two economists – Guglielmo Barone and Sauro Mocetti of the Bank of Italy – looked at tax returns in Florence for 1427 and 2011. They found that the occupations, income and wealth of families in 1427 were good predictors of the occupation, income and wealth of the same families nearly 600 years later.[1] This shows that having the right parents loads the dice in your favour in terms of wealth; however, it says nothing about whether you are a good leader or not. You can win the lottery and become rich, but that does not mean you can lead.

Further evidence also suggests that choosing the right DNA helps you reach the top. Research shows that the average height of a Fortune 500 CEO is 1.83 metres, versus an average for American males of about 1.77 metres.[2] There are two question marks about this research. The first is that it is based on what CEOs claim to be their height: 183 cm just happens to be six feet tall and a suspiciously large number claim to be six feet tall, not 5'11" or 5'10".

US presidents show the same height pattern. Here are the heights of the last few presidents:[3]

- Ronald Reagan   185cm
- George H Bush   188cm
- Bill Clinton   188cm
- George W Bush   182cm
- Barack Obama   185cm
- Donald Trump   191cm
- Joe Biden   182cm

The more important objection is that being a CEO, or even being president, does not mean that you are a leader; it means that you are very good at career management or at getting elected, which are different skills altogether. It is for you to decide which US presidents have been effective leaders, and whether height has anything to do with it.

So if you want a stellar career, it helps to choose the right DNA or bolster your shoes to gain height. It also helps, overwhelmingly, to be white and male if you want to succeed in a European or American context. If you want to succeed in a Japanese firm, it helps to be male and Japanese; in a Chinese context, it helps to be Chinese and male. The pattern is obvious.

It appears that social background and DNA will help you succeed in your career, but it says nothing about whether you will be a good leader once you reach the top.

Why this myth matters

If we do believe that leaders are born, not bred, then most people may as well give up. Believing that leaders can be bred is more constructive. It means that we all have a chance of becoming a leader. And in reality, we all can learn to lead. Learning to lead is like learning to play the piano. A little effort and rehearsal will make us better than most people who never even try. We may not have the patience, dedication and talent to become a famous soloist playing at Carnegie Hall, but we can all learn to lead better.

Lessons for leaders

Having a successful career and being a good leader are not the same thing. While historically, being born into the right family had a lot to do with leadership, the talent pool nowadays is far deeper, and the competition far greater. Merit has a lot more to do with things.

Believing that leaders are bred, not born, is essential for two reasons:

- *Pay and rewards*. Believing that success is based on merit is vital. If success is not based on merit, then there is no reason to pay top leaders outsized salaries, stock options, bonuses and deferred compensation. Without merit, leaders simply become lucky lottery winners.

- *Trust.* If people believe that leaders are not there on the basis of merit, then the leaders will not be trusted. Why would you trust someone simply because of their bloodline, or who had succeeded through luck alone? Trust in elites is evaporating fast.[4] If leaders are not trusted, it becomes very hard for them to lead. Merit, trust and leadership walk hand in hand.

But merit is only part of the picture – there is also the question of luck. While many leaders like to believe that luck is not a factor, the reality is that luck matters. That is not just the view of the also-rans who nearly made it, and blame bad luck for their lack of success. More reflective leaders often say things like: 'Of course, I have been very lucky... but I have made my luck.' The difference between failure and success is often very small. A contract or a promotion can go one way or the other: success is on a knife edge.

Napoleon famously liked lucky generals, until he met Wellington. He was right. He understood that leadership luck is not random. Leaders make their own luck. So how do you make your own luck? Here is how you can become the luckiest leader alive – all you have to do is acquire the three Ps of leadership: persistence, practice and perspective.[5]

Persistence

Leaders, like entrepreneurs, get used to the feeling of failure. Except that they never see it as failure; each setback is just another step on the path to success. They have an unquenchable belief in themselves and their mission. Churchill was a serial political failure. He described the 20 years between the two world wars as his 'wilderness years'.

Twenty years as an outcast would crush most people, but he kept going. In 1940, he became Prime Minister and discovered his finest hour at the age of 66. Often the difference between failure and success is as simple as not giving up.

Practice

Legendary golf champion Arnold Palmer once remarked: 'The harder I practise, the luckier I get.'[6] This is true. An amateur might hole a five-metre putt 20 per cent of the time; with practice, the 20 per cent chance becomes a 40 per cent chance, and eventually the highly practised professional might succeed 90 per cent of the time. With practice, the lucky shot becomes the skilled shot.

Practice is more than persistence. Persistence means keeping going. Practice means learning from experience, both good and bad. It is not enough to have deep experience; you have to learn from experience as well.

We can all learn to lead, and we can all learn to lead better even if we never become a global star in terms of leadership. To do this, we have to work out:

- What we have to learn: what are the skills and aptitudes we need to build to be an effective leader? (See Myth 8.)
- How we can learn it: what resources do we have to help us on our leadership journey? (See Myth 28.)

Perspective

Try this exercise. Think of all the bad things that happened today: inconsiderate drivers, traffic lights against you, annoying emails; tedious meetings. So are you lucky? Now think of all the good things that have happened. Simply to wake up in a warm house, with hot and cold running water, largely free from the fear of war, disease and famine makes us lottery winners in the field of human history. Our ancestors would envy us. So are you now lucky or unlucky? Sometimes luck is simply a matter of how we choose to feel.

Perspective is also about spotting opportunities. The reality is that we are surrounded by opportunity, but we only see it if we are looking for it. In one famous experiment, viewers were asked to observe how many times a basketball was passed between stationary players on court. During the video, someone in a gorilla suit walked on, danced around the players and walked off. Fewer than one quarter of the viewers saw the gorilla: most refused to believe that there had been a gorilla there. They were too busy counting passes.[7]

Within any firm there are always crises, new opportunities and moments of uncertainty and ambiguity. If you are looking for them, you will find them. And for entrepreneurs, the world is full of opportunity, if you have the courage to take up the challenge.

Of course, all leaders are lucky, because they make their luck.

Conclusion

The second paragraph of the American Declaration of Independence states: 'We hold these truths to be self-evident, that all men are created equal.'[8] Ideally, this would be true. The evidence shows it is false: your social background has a huge influence on your ability to get into a leadership position. But being successful and being a leader are different ideas. Leaders succeed on merit (with a bit of luck – which they make themselves – thrown in).

Notes

1   J Zumbrun. The wealthy in Florence are the same families as 600 years ago, *Wall Street Journal*, 2016, www.wsj.com/articles/the-wealthy-in-florence-today-are-the-same-families-as-600-years-ago-1463662410 (archived at https://perma.cc/87MT-FXQN)

2   B Daniels. Why many CEOs are tall people? The heart of the matter, Premium Times, 2016, www.premiumtimesng.com/entertainment/naija-fashion/203429-many-ceos-tall-people-height-matter-bisi-daniels.html (archived at https://perma.cc/GNE4-2YJS)

3   Wikipedia. Heights of presidents and presidential candidates of the United States, 2022, https://en.wikipedia.org/wiki/Heights_of_presidents_and_presidential_candidates_of_the_United_States (archived at https://perma.cc/Q6A3-V5MD). Note that Donald Trump's height is disputed.

4   Ipsos MORI veracity index 2021, www.ipsos.com/en-uk/ipsos-mori-veracity-index-trust-police-drops-second-year-row (archived at https://perma.cc/V7YB-9GPD)

5   This section draws on the research in Richard Wiseman's 2004 book, *The Luck Factor: The scientific study of the lucky mind*, Arrow Paperbacks, London

6   This is also attributed to Gary Player and Jerry Barber among many others. Regardless of who said it first, it remains a relevant comment.

7   There are many versions of this exercise, involving gorillas, storm troopers and moonwalking bears. For example: D Simons. Selective attention test, YouTube, 2010, www.youtube.com/watch?v=vJG698U2Mvo (archived at https://perma.cc/W5JJ-3PSU)

8   To be fair to the Founding Fathers, they probably did not intend to say that all people are born with equal life chances, but that they are equal before the law and equal as human beings.

Leaders are honest

It is not enough to be an honest leader; you have to be the trusted leader.

From an early age, children are taught that honesty is good and dishonesty is bad. It is a principle that pervades everyday life, and is at the heart of the law and a civilized society. We expect our fellow citizens to be honest and we certainly expect our leaders to be. The repeated failure of our political leaders to be honest is the source of endless scandal and media headlines.

Research on leadership showed that honesty was one of the top five expectations that followers had of their leaders.[1] It was also the most divisive expectation. Leaders either scored very high or very low: there was no middle ground. Leaders who were rated high on honesty had a chance of doing well on other leadership criteria. Leaders who scored low on honesty were trashed on every other criterion. No one liked working for a dishonest boss.

Why this myth matters

Given that honesty is so important, it is worth understanding what people mean by honesty. An implausible interview with a senior investment banker revealed the essence of the challenge. I sat down in his plush office with the fake antiques and here is our conversation:

Banker: 'Honesty has nothing to do with ethics or morality.'

Me: '??!!#?!'

Banker: 'It is far more important than that. Honesty is about trust. If my team does not trust me, then they will walk across the road tomorrow. If my clients don't trust me, then I will have no clients. A banker with no team and no clients is no use. Trust is everything.'

Trust requires hard-form honesty: it is not just the absence of lies, but the ability to say it as it is, all the time. It is not enough to be an honest leader: you have to be the trusted leader.

This ties in with the idea of authentic leadership (introduced in Myth 3). In Myth 3 we focused on the side of authentic leadership that states leaders should be true to who they are. Here we'll consider the other side of authentic leadership: that leaders should be open about their thoughts and beliefs. If you are to be trusted, you have to be honest. That means being honest about what you think. But as you think of your personal as well as professional life, there are plenty of times when being honest can cause problems. Discretion can be better than honesty.

The tension between honesty and discretion was high-lighted by one CEO who was reflecting on his leadership journey:

> When I was young I used to get angry and frustrated, and I showed it. It always got me into trouble. I still get angry and frustrated, but I have learned to wear the mask of leadership. My team picks up their mood from me. If I want them to be professional and positive, that is the mask I have to wear at all times. My mask has made all the difference.

Lessons for leaders

Should you be open and honest about your thoughts and beliefs all the time? If your thoughts are always positive and constructive, you are fortunate and you have the foundations of being a very good leader. Most of the time, most of us can stay positive and constructive. But most of the time does not count. We do not want to have a heart which works 'most of the time'. The moment of truth is when things are going awry: how do you react then?

This is where being open and honest is dangerous. You need to be open and honest about the situation because people want to know what is going on and where they stand. This approach builds trust. But if you are feeling angry, frustrated and vengeful then being open and honest about that is destructive and will not help you to build trust. It will cause your team to implode in a mixture of fear and finger pointing. It is at these times you need to wear your mask of leadership: project the style which you want your team to follow.

You need to be careful even with your thoughts. From time to time you may think that someone has been idle, careless, dishonest or plain foolish. If you are open with these thoughts to that individual, and to others, you have a recipe for conflict. And it may even be that your initial judgement is wrong; there are often plenty of innocent explanations for mishaps. Sometimes, instead of being authentic, it pays to be discreet. Keep your views to yourself; buy some time to allow you to find out what really happened and remember that the number one goal is to be trusted.

Over the years, a simple formula has shown the way to building trust. Here it is:

$$t = \frac{(i \times c)}{(s \times r)}$$

Where:

t = trust
i = intimacy
c = credibility
s = selfishness
r = risk

This is how you put the trust equation into practice, so that you can become the trusted leader.

Intimacy

This is about having common values, common experiences, common outlook and a common agenda with your counterpart. It is both style and substance.

In style terms, we all find it easier to work with someone like ourselves, because we understand how they think and operate. One of the challenges of global teams is that there is too much distance between team members who do not understand how the other members think. This is one reason why people often appear to waste time gossiping about trivia when they first meet. The gossip has a purpose: they are trying to find common ground in terms of experiences and outlook. It is the first building block of building personal trust between strangers.

In terms of substance, intimacy means sharing a common agenda and common goal. This should be self-evident. We will find it easier to cooperate if we have a common need, or even a common enemy, than if we are working on competing agendas. In practice, it is often hard to find out what the mutual need is. In particular, when selling or negotiating, a large part of the art is to discover the other side's agenda. When you know what their needs, wants and fears are it is much easier to find the win–win solution.

Credibility

Most of us have friends who would score highly on intimacy, but we would not trust them to do anything important. They score low on credibility. Credibility is about always doing what you say, 100 per cent of the time. Credibility is hard to build and easy to lose. Like a vase, once it is broken it is very hard to put back together and is never quite the same.

Most of us like to believe we do as we say. Perhaps we do. But what we think we say is not the same as what other people think they hear. Messages always get scrambled. We may say things like:

- 'I hope to...'
- 'I will try...'
- 'I will see if...'

What the other side hears is 'I will...'. When we then come back and say we tried (but did not deliver) we will have lost trust. There is no point in arguing about what was or was not said. Perceptions may be false, but the consequences of perceptions are real. This means that we have to be brutally clear in what we say and we have to make sure that we have been understood.

Credibility requires 100 per cent delivery and very clear communication.

Selfishness

We are all heroes of our own life story, and the universe revolves around our own reality. But the more we put ourselves first, the less other people will want to work with us and for us. Even the best leaders ultimately put themselves first. But they also have an ability to understand and respect the needs and wants of others.

Risk

Risk is like kryptonite to trust. The riskier the situation, the more trust is required. I may trust a stranger to tell me the way to the post office. I would be unwise to trust the stranger with my life savings. Risk matters. You can manage risk two ways: reduce the risk or raise the risk.

Reducing risk is obvious, up to a point. Risk is not the abstract risk that exists in risk logs. It is personal risk: will I be able to do this, will I look like a fool if it goes wrong, will I still have a job at the end of it? This is the sort of risk you need to manage as a leader. Reduce the challenge into bite-sized chunks which make it less risky and provide the right support. De-risk the future.

The less obvious route to managing risk is to raise it. Show that the risks of doing nothing are greater than the risks of change. This is where leaders often create the 'burning platform' story. They show that the business is burning down and that without radical action everything will be lost.

Conclusion

Honesty is vital as part of trust. Trust is the number one goal, and sometimes, it doesn't pay to be completely honest about your thoughts and beliefs. Keep your sights on building trust. Trust is asymmetric: we know others can trust us, but we are not sure we can trust others. This means that in practice many leaders fall at the trust hurdle. Leaders are (mostly) honest, but struggle to build trust.

Note

1   Author's original interviews with leaders and their teams.

The best leaders are clever: They should be the smartest person in the room

*If you want to be a leader, trust your team
to take on every challenge.*

This is another bargain two-for-the-price-of-one myth. It has two elements:

1 Leaders are clever.
2 Leaders are smarter than everyone else.

Leaders are clever

First, let's differentiate between being academically clever and being smart. Academic leadership is an oxymoron: a room full of PhDs will generate debate, not leadership. No one ever accused Einstein of being a great leader. If you turn to today's top billionaires, most of them are an MBA-free zone and about half of them did not complete university. But it would be unwise to call Zuckerberg, Gates or Brin dumb: they are clearly very smart.

From time immemorial, communities have craved the wise leader who could dispense justice and uphold the law. The advent of the Industrial Revolution took this idea forward. New-fangled factories needed to be organized by smart leaders and run by workers who were essentially unreliable cogs in the machine. Ideas had to flow out of the heads of the bosses and into the hands of the workers: bosses had the brains and workers had the hands.

In today's world, everyone is better educated. Education is a necessary but insufficient criterion for success. Smart leadership is very different from the past.

Why this myth matters

If you are to succeed as a leader, it helps to know what skills and capabilities you need for success. The nature of leadership is changing, because the nature of the firm and the workforce is changing. The two major changes are:

1 The workforce is smarter than ever, and will only get smarter in the future. This has two implications for leaders:
   ◦ What sort of smartness do you need in order to lead when everyone else is also smart?
   ◦ How do you lead people who probably want less management but have higher expectations than ever before?

2 Firms are outsourcing, downsizing, flattening out and specializing like never before. This means that leaders no longer control either all the people or all the resources they need to succeed. So how do you lead when you no longer have direct control?

Lessons for leaders

The smart leader today requires three sets of skills, which we can label IQ, EQ and PQ.

IQ: INTELLIGENCE QUOTIENT

An intelligent leader is likely to do better than a dumb leader. But management intelligence is different from academic intelligence. Academic intelligence is about slowly accumulating a body of knowledge over time. Management intelligence has two elements:

1 *Recognizing patterns fast and reacting to them.* Leaders have to identify patterns in all the ambiguous situations they encounter and learn from them, so that next time they encounter a similar situation they know what to do.
2 *Learning and adapting to new situations fast.* Pattern recognition does not always work, because you will inevitably encounter unfamiliar situations. When faced with crises, uncertainty or ambiguity, managers will step back and leaders will step up. The more often the leader steps up, the more they learn about how to step up successfully.

EQ: EMOTIONAL QUOTIENT

Given that the workforce is now better educated than ever, leaders have to lead differently. It is not enough to be the leader that people have to follow. You need to be the leader that people *want* to follow. This means treating people as people, not as cogs in a machine. Smart EQ is about motivating people, building balanced teams, developing talent and managing yourself and your own emotions well. EQ requires understanding how you affect other people and adapting appropriately.

PQ: POLITICAL QUOTIENT

You can find plenty of nice (high EQ) and smart (high IQ) people who languish in the backwaters of the firm. They are used by more ruthless colleagues as doormats on the path to success. Clearly, something is missing in the success formula. In the 21st century, the nature of leadership has changed. Firms have hollowed out and flattened. Leaders no longer control all the resources they need. Instead, they have to:

- persuade colleagues
- build networks of influence and trust within and beyond the firm
- align agendas and find allies for their projects
- fight for resources, which means that your real competition is not in the market: it is your colleague sharing a video call with you
- find the right bosses, projects and experiences to succeed

These 21st century skills are deeply political. They are about making the organization work with you and for you. Leaders with these political skills have high PQ: political quotient.

Leaders may still need to be smart, but the nature of smartness is changing, and they need other skills as well. Today, leaders need IQ, EQ and PQ skills. The performance bar rises all the time.

Leaders are smarter than everyone else

This myth is closely related to two leadership theories: the Great Man theory of leadership (in which the leader believes they are smarter than everyone) and the idea of humble leadership. Both these myths are introduced in Myth 3.

Hierarchy replicates the parent–child relationship: the boss is the parent and the team member is the child.[1] This creates unhealthy tension in the team. In practice, it means that many teams are very good at delegating: they like to delegate all the problems up to the leader. This relieves them of accountability for the solution. It also allows them to complain that the boss has made the wrong decision in the wrong way, and that the boss is really a complete idiot, just like teenagers complaining about their gormless parents. Inevitably, the boss is the last person to hear of these complaints. To your face, the team will be polite and supportive because they know their future is in your hands.

The boss is complicit in this game. The boss may be a benevolent or abusive parent, but the dynamic is the same. The boss often feels the need to prove their worth. They want to show they can handle the toughest problems; they want to be seen to be smart and in control. They want to be the adult in the room and they want to look good.

This is a game which gets played out in all parts of the firm, even at the highest levels. The essential parent–child script never really changes. Inevitably, 40-year-old adults resent being treated like children, but that is the role that the script of the hierarchy forces on them.

Why this myth matters

The parent–child script is highly dysfunctional, because it:

- *Disempowers*. By letting delegation flow up to the parent boss, the team is disempowered. If it does not take decisions, then it cannot be held accountable. That makes performance management extremely hard.
- *Disables*. A high-performing team is one that is challenged and stretched, not one which lives life in the slow lane. By letting the team delegate upwards, the team avoids the toughest challenges. In the short term, this is often the easy way out. If the boss knows what to do, then let the boss do it. But in the long term it is the road to under-achievement: the team will never learn and never develop.
- *Demotivates*. A team which is disempowered and not developing will lose motivation, even if in the short-term life in the comfort zone is comfortable. Lack of delegation from the boss shows lack of trust and confidence in the ability of the team. This then sets up a vicious circle. As the team loses motivation, confidence and performance go down. This signals to the leader that the team cannot be entrusted with vital work, so the leader takes on an increasing burden. This then further disempowers, disables and demotivates the team.

- *Overwhelms.* By delegating everything upwards, the team leader takes on an increasing burden which is eventually overwhelming. If you want to be heroic, take on every challenge yourself. If you want to be a leader, trust your team to take on every challenge.

Lessons for leaders

Here are the top six lessons for leaders from this myth.

BE HUMBLE ABOUT YOURSELF

As a leader, your role is not to become indispensable; your role is to make yourself dispensable. Build your team and your firm so that it has the strength to thrive without you.

Research on 69,000 managers' 360-degree feedback shows that leaders either overestimate or underestimate their capabilities: no surprise there.[2] But the leaders who underestimate their capabilities are seen to be better leaders by their teams. Teams engage better with a humble leader than an overbearing one. Teams also rate humble leaders as being more effective. This is a subjective rating: teams rate leaders they like highly.

In practice, this sort of humility is hard to come by. Most of us have a superiority complex. Here are some examples:

- Eighty-seven per cent of Stanford MBA students rated themselves as above average.[3]
- Of 1 million students sitting SAT exams, 85 per cent thought they were above average in ability to get on with others; 25 per cent thought they were in the top 1 per cent.[4]

- Ninety-three per cent of drivers thought they had above-average driving skills; even among the modest Swedes, 69 per cent thought they were above average.[5]

Now test yourself: do you think you are below or above average in terms of honesty, reliability, hard work, decency and driving ability? Most of us think we are above average, which is statistically impossible but emotionally inevitable.

The benefit of being humble about your own abilities is that it encourages you to learn and grow, as well as respect the views and talents of other people. It makes you more inclusive on decision making, and more willing to delegate. These are useful traits for a leader to have.

KNOW YOUR ROLE

The role of the leader is not to be the smartest person in the room. The role of the leader is to get the smartest people in the room. The coach of a sports team is very rarely the best player; the coach is the person who finds and develops the best players for the team. Once you do this, you can value each person for their unique talents and contribution and you can start to move away from the parent–child script.

CHANGE THE SCRIPT

Change the script with your team. Move from the parent–child script to the adult–adult script. At the heart of this is a revolutionary idea: ignore the hierarchy. Instead of thinking like boss–team member, simply think of the team where each person has a different and vital role to play. The team leader has a role to play in coaching, setting direction and managing resources, but each team player has a vital role to play as well. You all have an equal contribution to make and no one is better than anyone else: each contribution is simply different.

ENFORCE ACCOUNTABILITY

Do not let your team delegate upwards to you. Delegation should work the other way around. You should be finding ways in which to stretch and challenge your team with meaningful work. In a parent–child script, the leader always lands up with all the accountability. This leaves the team members disempowered and resentful. In an adult–adult script, everyone is equal and everyone has different roles and accountability: each person is empowered. This normally raises morale and performance, and it makes performance management easier because it is clear who is accountable for what.

PAY MORE ATTENTION TO YOUR TEAM

As a manager and leader it is natural to spend most time thinking about how to manage your boss. We spend more time looking up, not down, the hierarchy. This makes sense, because your boss can control your fate. Bosses do not come with a user manual, so it takes real effort to work out how to influence your boss. But the result is that leaders often do not spend as much time thinking deeply about how to influence each team member. But if you are the coach of your team, you can only get top performance if you act like a coach who is dedicated to helping each team member improve.

TRUST YOUR TEAM

Failure to delegate reflects lack of trust in your team, and your team knows that. Show confidence in your team, and your trust will normally be repaid handsomely. Most people want to do well and want to show that they can be trusted with important challenges. Don't let the buck stop with you: pass the buck down. Let your team rise to the challenge, and then watch them grow in confidence and capability.

Conclusion

There is a difference between being academically clever and being smart. The smartest leaders have high IQ, EQ and PQ skills. These skills help leaders to realize that they do not need to be the smartest person in the room. But this myth runs deep. The result? Many leaders struggle because they fail to delegate or trust their team properly. Even if the leader genuinely is the smartest person in the room, it can pay to introduce a little humility. That being said, believing that you are the smartest person in the room is not fatal to a leadership career. This is a myth which cripples rather than kills the leader.

Notes

1   This section is based on transactional analysis. See E Berne (1964) *Games People Play: The psychology of human relations*, 1978 reprint, Grove Press, New York

2   J Zenger and J Folkman. We like leaders who underrate themselves, *Harvard Business Review*, November 2015, https://hbr.org/2015/11/ we-like-leaders-who-underrate-themselves (archived at https://perma.cc/ VWM6-HNGY)

3   E W Zuckerman and J Jost. What makes you think you're so popular? Self-evaluation maintenance and the subjective side of the 'Friendship Paradox', *Social Psychology Quarterly*, 2001, 64 (3), 207–23

4   M Alicke, D Dunning and J Krueger (2005) *The Self in Social Judgement*, Psychology Press, London, 85–106

5   O Svenson. Are we all less risky and more skillful than our fellow drivers? *Acta Psychologica*, 1981, 47 (2), 143–48

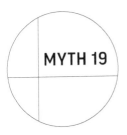

Male and female leaders are different

*Respect people for who they are, not for their
DNA or chromosomes.*

A good way to sell books and get media attention is to show that men and women lead in fundamentally different ways: 'Men are from Mars, Women are from Venus' is not just the message; it is also the title of a bestselling book.[1]

Research may be more boring, but is also more useful. Even in a post-truth world, it can pay to act on the basis of evidence as opposed to belief. The research is nuanced.[2] There are differences, but not as dramatic as the popular press might want to show. An early landmark meta-analysis by Professor Alice Eagly found that in real organizational life, the differences between male and female stereotypes were small.[3] In laboratory conditions, the stereotypes became more pronounced. The standard stereotypes between male and female leaders are shown in Table 19.1. You can add or subtract your own views of gender stereotypes to the table.

A different way of looking at the debate is to ask how far the genders differ on each factor. The two diagrams

TABLE 19.1 Male and female leadership stereotypes

Female leadership stereotypes	Male leadership stereotypes
People focus	Task focus
Participative/democratic	Directive/autocratic
Cautious	Risk taking
Less assertive	More assertive
Emotionally aware	Focus on the facts

FIGURE 19.1 Stereotypical view of gender differences

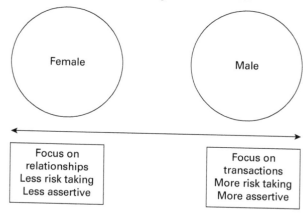

FIGURE 19.2 Research-based view of gender differences

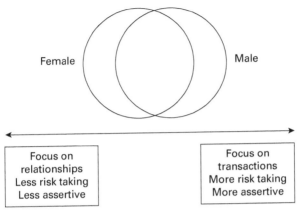

above show how you can think about gender differences. Figure 19.1 shows how the popular press like to portray the differences: men and women are literally from different planets.

Figure 19.2 shows how the research portrays the differences between genders. It shows that there are differences, but they are not a clean split on gender lines. You can find plenty of men who have more of the female stereotypical traits, and plenty of women who have more of the male stereotypical traits.

Why this myth matters

Gender differences, or lack of them, matter from at least three perspectives.

Building a balanced leadership team

Clearly, if the popular view of gender differences is accurate then that has major implications for picking and developing leaders. It would mean that some leadership roles should be the sole preserve of women, and others should be the sole preserve of men. Some roles require high risk taking (male) while others require excellent interpersonal skills (women).

If the reality is more nuanced, you will still need a balanced team in terms of styles. The gender stereotypes illustrate a few of the major style differences, but they are not the only ones.

Developing leaders of the future

If there are gender differences, then one-size-fits-all leadership development can lead to very unequal outcomes, as illustrated by the experience of Future Leaders (see box below).

BUILDING LEADERS OF THE FUTURE

Future Leaders was a project designed to fast track outstanding talent into leadership of schools in the toughest areas. Its intake broadly reflected the population of middle managers in schools: it was 50/50 female/male.

After about five years, we found that 80 per cent of the people who had been promoted to head teacher were male. This was not the outcome we expected or wanted.

We looked at what was going wrong. Unsurprisingly, we found women faced significant hurdles:

- conscious or unconscious sexism from selection panels
- the buggy in the hallway: women were still finding that they were doing most of the home making and child minding

We also found the genders living up (or down) to their stereotypes. Typically, men would start applying for posts even when we knew they were only 40–50 per cent ready. They would try to blag their way through, confident that if they got the job they would rise to the challenge. If they were rejected, their view was that the selection panel had made a mistake. They ignored the feedback from each panel. This meant they would keep on trying, and eventually they would land a role.

In contrast, the women waited until they knew they would be able to do the job. Even when we knew they were 80 per cent ready (and no one is ever 100 per cent ready to step up to a new role), they had to be encouraged to apply. If they were rejected, they would take the feedback from the selection panel seriously, meaning they would not apply again until they felt they had addressed the weaknesses the selection panel claimed to have found.

Men were pushing themselves forward; women were holding themselves back. In the following five years, the programme was adjusted to reflect the different approaches of each gender and eventually the promotions to headship achieved a gender balance.

Public policy

The gender debate will continue for many decades. It is for you to decide how far the stereotypes are true and what should be done about them: this book focuses on the implications for you as a leader.

Lessons for leaders

Below are four lessons we can draw.

Build a balanced team

The different stereotypes highlight the need to achieve a balanced leadership team. If the whole team is made up of risk junkies, it may succeed fast but it is also likely to crash fast. Achieving a balance of talents and styles is vital.

Understand your own style

Regardless of your gender, it is worth thinking about how far you are task focused or people focused; democratic or autocratic; risk taking and assertive or cautious and supportive. It is usual to say that there is no wrong or right style, but that is misleading. Universally, there may be no wrong or right style, but in your specific context there will be a style which works better than others. You have to find a context to work in which your style succeeds.

Promotions do not go to the meek

The story of Future Leaders shows that you have to be prepared to push yourself. Don't wait until you are

100 per cent confident you can step up, because you can never be 100 per cent ready for your next role.

Respect people for who they are

Perhaps the most important lesson for leaders is to respect people for who they are, not for their DNA or chromosomes. How far we should discriminate in favour of one group (and by implication against another group) on the basis of their DNA is a public policy matter on which everyone will have their views.

Conclusion

We live in a post-truth world where people believe what they want to believe. There clearly are gender differences, but there is disagreement about how great the differences are, whether they matter, and what should be done about it.

Notes

1   J Gray (1992) *Men Are From Mars, Women Are From Venus: A practical guide for improving communication and getting what you want in your relationships*, HarperCollins, London

2   HBR has a good overview here: A Eagly and L Carli (2007) *Through the Labyrinth: The truth about how women become leaders*, Harvard Business School Press, Boston, 130–131

3   A Eagly and B Johnson, Gender and leadership style: A meta-analysis, *Psychological Bulletin*, 1990, 108 (2)

Psychopaths succeed as leaders

Being charming, violent and lacking empathy are all part of the same package.

Psychopaths are generally seen as mad, bad and dangerous to know. Psychopaths are regular customers of prisons around the world. They are 25 times more likely to land up in prison than the rest of the population.[1] At first sight, this is not the obvious profile of a leader.

Research estimates that about 1 per cent of the population (mainly male) is strongly or moderately psychopathic.[2] Between 3 and 21 per cent of senior corporate officials are rated as psychopaths.[3] The wide divergence of estimates reflects ambiguity about who qualifies as a psychopath. There are many varying degrees of psychopathy: everyone has an element of the psychopath within them. In any event, it is clear that psychopaths are disproportionately good at getting themselves into trouble; they are also disproportionately good at getting themselves into power.

Why this myth matters

If psychopaths succeed as leaders, then there must be things we can learn from them about the nature of leadership. So it makes sense to understand what the main characteristics of a psychopath are:[4]

- bold and self-confident
- stress tolerant
- risk taking
- charming and charismatic

These are all good qualities for any leader to have. If you are to take people where they would not have got by themselves, you have to take risks, endure high stress, be bold and engage people enthusiastically in your mission. These are also traits which work well in particular types of work. Traders at large banks need the qualities of the psychopath as listed above. Perhaps if investment banks test for psychopaths, it is not to weed them out but to select them in. The film *Wall Street* and subsequent scandals would indicate that some investment banks may have been selecting on this basis, accidentally or otherwise.

So why do psychopaths get such a bad name? Because they also have traits from the dark side. They are:

- amoral
- lacking in any empathy

- manipulative
- violent

Not all of these traits appear to be consistent; how can someone lack empathy but be charming? The answer is that psychopaths are very good at reading people. They will find your motivations, hopes and fears fast, and then they will play on them. This can appear empathetic, but it is a performance; they turn their show of interest on and off like flicking a switch. They appear to be charming, but they are simply manipulating. Less educated psychopaths have less ability to manipulate through charm or to intimidate through words. Instead, they will seek to manipulate and intimidate through violence: that is how so many land up in prison. Being charming, violent and lacking empathy are all part of the same package.

The ability to manipulate enables psychopaths to work their way up through an organization. Their self-confidence to take risks and make bold decisions can help them become leaders who make a difference. But their success comes at a price: they are often divisive, destructive and amoral. They are natural dictators within your firm, and natural dictators of nations.

THE PSYCHOPATH IN ACTION

Lee did not care for working for bosses he regarded as weak and foolish. So he told the partners that he would start a new practice based on advising oil and gas companies. Since none of the partners worked in this area, they let him get on with it.

Lee was very ambitious. He worked hard and soon got clients eating out of his hand. He could charm them, and he made sure they got high-quality work by building a devoted team. He demanded 100 per cent loyalty from them, but he gave 100 per cent loyalty in return. In return for working all hours, Lee consistently delivered outsized bonuses and promotions to his team. Anyone who showed just 99 per cent loyalty was ejected and trashed. Anyone who dared opposed him was squashed: no one dared to stand up to him.

In effect, Lee had set up his own business which played to its own rules: Lee's rules. There were dark stories about how success was achieved, but as long as the profits flowed the questions were not too searching.

Lessons for leaders

Seek to understand, not to judge

Moral indignation is a natural reaction to finding that psychopaths succeed. But what is natural is not always good: floods, earthquakes, death and disease are all quite natural. Instead of judging psychopaths, understand them. That way you can learn from them, you can learn how to spot them, and you can learn how to deal with them or avoid them.

Look in the mirror

We all have psychopathic tendencies, both good and bad. At times of great pressure and stress, even decent people will put themselves first. It is easy to appear amoral, to be trying to manipulate people, facts and events, and to have less empathy than is ideal.

Beware psychopaths

They are highly manipulative. They know how to lie and how to fight, because they have plenty of practice. You are unlikely to win a fight against them because you have less experience. So you have a choice. Either you can sign up and support them: the best psychopaths know they need a good team and will be very loyal to you... for just as long as they have use for you; or you can steer well clear of them and find better colleagues to work with.

Avoid labels

Calling someone a psychopath is an easy insult, but insults do not help. Leave the diagnosis to the medical world, although even they struggle to agree on who qualifies as a psychopath.

Beware your firm

Most firms have the character of a psychopath: they have no empathy and, by themselves, they are quite amoral. Constant corporate scandals show how firms can be amoral. Normal working and environmental conditions in many emerging economy firms show that morality and empathy do not rate highly. Firms, like psychopaths, will support you and be loyal to you in return for your loyalty and commitment... until they decide they no longer need you.

Conclusion

This myth is built on a large dose of reality. Being a psychopath is good for getting into leadership positions, but does not necessarily make you a good leader.

Notes

1 K A Kiehl and M B Hoffman. The criminal psychopath: History, neuroscience, treatment, and economics, *Jurimetrics*, Summer 2011, 51, 355–97

2 P Babiak and R D Hare (2007) *Snakes in Suits: When psychopaths go to work*, HarperBusiness, New York

3 See K Frtizon, N Brooks and S Croom (2020) *Investigating Destructive Personalities in the Workplace*, Palgrave Macmillan, London

4 R D Hare and C N Neumann (2006) The PCL-R assessment of psychopathy: Development, structural properties, and new directions, in C Patrick (ed), *Handbook of Psychopathy*, Guilford, 58–88

MYTH 21

Leaders are reasonable

The world was never changed by reasonable people.

To tell someone that they are being unreasonable is an insult. As a society, we value reason. The 18th century witnessed the Enlightenment, which was also called the Age of Reason. It was the era when scientific method finally displaced religious belief as a way of explaining and exploring the world. It was the moment when Europe started to make huge progress in knowledge and technology, paving the way for the Industrial Revolution and transforming society. Reason was the mark of civilization. Leaders were meant to be well educated and able to command reason. Reason stood at the heart of society and of leadership.

The power of reason moved directly into business with the rise of Scientific Management, with Frederick Taylor in the vanguard of the movement. Nowadays his methods are seen as being little more than time and motion, but that is unfair. He always took account of the human element in a very logical way, and his methods transformed productivity. They found expression in Henry Ford's revolutionary moving production line for cars which transformed the auto industry.

Leadership is still based on reason. IT systems become more powerful all the time and produce more data than ever before. There is an insatiable appetite for data to help leaders gain insights and make more informed decisions. Strategy consultants produce volumes of data to justify their findings. An age of hyper data is also an age of hyper reason.

So it looks like case closed: leaders need reason and logic and they need to be reasonable. Anyone who is unreasonable is seen to be wild, unpredictable and very difficult to work with.

No leader wants to be unreasonable, do they?

Why this myth matters

The best leaders are not reasonable. They understand that when you accept reason, you accept failure: there are always reasons why something cannot be achieved, why a deadline must be put back, why a target should be lowered. There is always a reason you should not chase your dream.

The world was never changed by reasonable people. Great empires are not built on reason, whether they are territorial empires or business empires.

ALEXANDER THE REASONABLE?

Alexander the Great was born in a tin pot state on the edge of (Greek) civilization. If he had been reasonable, he would have fooled around in his state and pretended to be civilized: his father had hired Aristotle, the rock star philosopher of the day, to educate Alexander in an attempt to gain admission to the civilized world.

Alexander may have been tutored in logic and reason, but he was not reasonable. From his tin pot state he conquered the entire civilized world and beyond by the age of 30. As with endless conquerors since, he met his match in modern day Afghanistan.

Since then, he has always been known in the West as Alexander the Great. Meanwhile, who has ever heard of his cousin Alexander the Reasonable? Greatness and reasonableness do not sleep together.

In business, no one in their right mind would try to take on entrenched multi-billion-dollar businesses which have a monopoly on technology and market access. But people who have more belief than reason will do that, and they can succeed. In each case in Table 21.1, the incumbents would never have imagined that they would be threatened by today's challengers: either the challengers did not exist, or they were too small to worry about.

In many cases, the new challengers did not start with a detailed business plan. Ryanair started with one plane and an idea: it is now the largest European carrier in passenger numbers.[1] In every case, reason took a back seat to ambition.

The tension between reason and ambition is now reflected in strategic thinking. The traditional approach to strategy was dominated by pointy-headed analysts who would crunch data. This was the world of Michael Porter's five competitive forces,[2] and the BCG growth/share matrix. It was a world of charts and two-by-two matrices, where analysis would yield an insight into the future. It was a world Isaac Newton would have recognized: predictable action and reaction. Such a rational world might help slow-moving legacy firms; it did nothing to help disruptive upstarts who wanted to change the nature of competition itself.

C K Prahalad and Gary Hamel led the revolt against reason with their ideas of strategic intent and core competences.[3] They encouraged leaders to be bold, set audacious

TABLE 21.1 Challengers and incumbents

Challengers	Incumbents
Ryanair	British Airways
Sky/Fox	BBC/CBS
Tesla	Ford, GM
Dyson	Hoover
Amazon	Barnes & Noble
Spotify, Deezer, Tidal	Warner, Universal, Sony
Uber	Taxi firms
Google	Encyclopaedias, map-makers, classified ads, printed media

targets and then build the capability to achieve those goals, while fundamentally changing the terms of competition. They learned from David and Goliath: don't fight on the terms of the giant.

Leaders hate being called unreasonable or ruthless, but even the nicest leaders can be ruthless in achieving their goals. They might call it being 'hard edged' but if you are on the receiving end of the hard edge, it feels pretty ruthless.

HARD EDGED OR RUTHLESS?

Sarah and Anne had joined the school teaching staff at the same time, straight from university. They both progressed through the school, taking on ever-greater responsibilities. Over 20 years, they became firm friends. Their families would go on holiday together and they often had Sunday lunch together.

Eventually, Sarah was appointed head teacher. It was a popular appointment because the staff liked Sarah. Her friend Anne had been Head of the English department for several years.

Sarah took stock of the school and realized that if it was to perform properly for the children it served, it needed to refresh the staff pool. Several staff members were not good enough and were holding the school back. Anne held a crucial role as Head of English, and was one of the key people holding back performance. Sarah fired Anne, as nicely as she could.

That was a quick end to a long friendship. But school performance improved dramatically and Sarah was confident she had done the right thing: hard edged or ruthless?

Lessons for leaders

Leaders need to be selectively unreasonable. Managers need to be reasonable. Below are three areas where you may forget to be reasonable.

Be unreasonable about your ambition

A leader takes people where they would not have got by themselves. That means you have to dare to stretch people and to challenge them. Most people rise to the challenge, and they grow as a result.

Be ruthless in pursuing the dream

One of the core tasks of the leader is to create the team which can deliver the result. Ultimately, survival of the organization is more important than survival of the individual. If you have to move people off your team, then that is what you must do.

Ignore excuses

Neither accept excuses nor deny them. Excuses are dangerous for two reasons: they look backwards, not forwards, and they create a reason for not delivering. Instead of focusing on the excuse, focus on what needs to happen next, if the original goal is to be achieved on the original schedule.

WHAT WOULD YOU DO?

Penicillin was discovered in 1928, but it was hard to make in volume.[4] It was only during the Second World War that the Americans finally worked out how to produce large batches of the life-saving miracle drug.

An early batch found its way to Egypt, where it posed a problem for the British commanders. They could use it on thousands of service men who had been fooling around in the pleasure palaces of Cairo and Alexandria: a small dose would cure them and get them back to the front. Or they could use much more of it on a few wounded war heroes: some might die anyway, others might have lived anyway but it could make all the difference and save a few of them.

They cabled back to London to ask Churchill what they should do. Your call: save the wounded war heroes, or get the troops who had been fooling around back onto the front line?

Churchill's choice was clear: 'Use it for best military advantage'. Use it to get as many troops as possible back onto the front line. The goal was to defeat the enemy, not save the wounded.

When leaders have a very clear goal, they become ruthless in chasing it.

Conclusion

We may want reasonable leaders, but leaders have to be selectively unreasonable and ruthless to achieve their mission. They may be reasonable for 90 per cent of the time, but are unreasonable at the moments of truth.

Notes

1   Wikipedia. List of largest airlines in Europe, 2022, https://en.wikipedia.org/wiki/List_of_largest_airlines_in_Europe (archived at https://perma.cc/8YZ8-J5GU)
2   M E Porter. The five competitive forces that shape strategy, *Harvard Business Review*, January 2008, 86–104
3   G Hamel and C K Prahalad. Strategic intent, *Harvard Business Review*, 2005, https://hbr.org/2005/07/strategic-intent (archived at https://perma.cc/7G9J-3BGH)
4   American Chemical Society. Discovery and development of penicillin, nd, www.acs.org/content/acs/en/education/whatischemistry/landmarks/flemingpenicillin.html (archived at https://perma.cc/GZ6L-H3QU)

MYTH 22

The best leader is a skilled leader

The best leaders are not always the most skilled.

This myth permeates leadership development and leadership books. There are endless courses available which all deal with different aspects of leadership. At the heart of most leadership development is the belief that there are known skills and capabilities which can be defined, shared and learned by emerging leaders. The quality of these courses varies dramatically: some can be life changing. Others are a good opportunity to get up to date with your email backlog.

On balance, a skilled leader is more likely to be effective than an unskilled leader. But as you look at leaders you have encountered, it is obvious that all leaders have weaknesses, and not all leaders are the most skilled people in the firm. This is partly the result of the goldfish bowl effect: leaders live life in a goldfish bowl where every movement and every defect is seen and commentated upon. Life in the backwaters is quieter and any minor flaws you may have are not so obvious.

If the best leaders are not always the most skilled, then they must have something else. Is there an x-factor which separates out the best leaders from the rest?

Why this myth matters

Skills are necessary, but not sufficient for a leader. If we are to find the leaders of the future and help them emerge, we need to know what leaders need in addition to skills.

Research has shown that the best leaders act differently because they think differently.[1] That much is obvious. More surprising is that the way the best leaders think is consistent and is different from the standard corporate mindset. The best news is that these mindsets are not part of your DNA. They are simply habits of mind that anyone can learn in the same way anyone can learn any skill: practice makes you better even if you never become a superstar.

Lessons for leaders

Here are seven (plus one) mindsets which separate out the best leaders from the rest.

High aspirations

The corporate mindset interprets high aspirations as excellence. Keep improving and become best in class. Excellence is fine as far as it goes, which is not far enough. Leaders look beyond excellence to see what they can change: can they change the rules of the game, or find a fundamentally different way of working? This is about making a difference, which implies taking far greater risks than the corporate mindset allows.

Leaders who are deeply committed to a mission they believe in quickly develop the other mindsets. They find the courage to take risks, the resilience to overcome setbacks, and allies with whom they can collaborate to succeed. They remain relentlessly positive about doing something they believe in and they will be prepared to make the tough decisions which appear ruthless.

Courageous

If you are to take people where they would not have got by themselves, that means you will challenge orthodoxy, you will take people towards the unknown and you will meet resistance. It means taking risk, while the corporate mindset looks to manage risk. Leaders will take risks to start things and change things, step up at crises when others step back, challenge and fight battles where they have to.

Resilient

The nature of risk is that sometimes it does not succeed. If you have never failed, you have never taken enough risk: a risk which always works is not a risk. Most leaders succeed on the back of repeated failures and setbacks. This has a curious effect: the more you encounter setbacks, the better you become at dealing with them. If you never fail, you have no experience or resilience to fall back on.

Accountable

Corporate accountability is lopsided: take the praise and spread the blame. It is also limited to the formula where accountability = responsibility. Leaders see accountability differently in at least three ways:

- Seek responsibility beyond your narrow accountability. Build personal power through influence and networks of trust and support so that your power is not limited by your position.
- Spread the praise and shield the blame: the effect on team motivation and trust is transformational.
- Be accountable for your own feelings: wear the mask of leadership, not the mask of anger and frustration.

Positive

The corporate positive mindset is reduced on occasion to instructing staff to say 'Have a nice day' while thinking 'Please drop dead'. Being positive is not about telling people to have passion while you de-layer, right size, re-engineer and outsource operations. Being positive comes from within: find meaning in what you do; count your blessings; look to the future, don't dwell on the past; move to action, not analysis; see opportunities, not just problems.

Collaborative

The corporate rhetoric is about teamwork, but the corporate reality is that many managers find it hard to let go: delegating to the team and trusting peers is hard. The best leaders have the best teams. They are deeply collaborative because they have to be: they cannot do it all themselves. Having a great team enables each leader to focus their time and energy where they can most make a difference. Everything else can be delegated.

Growth

Leadership is a journey in which the context keeps changing and the rules of survival and success keep changing. This means leaders have to keep learning and adapting. It is not a craft skill like plumbing or the law where you have to master a known body of knowledge and skills (and then top them up over your career). You have to keep on refreshing your success model.

The 'plus one': Ruthless

This is the mindset from the dark side. Making a difference requires a hard edge: making tough decisions; having difficult (but constructive) conversations; setting high and stretching goals; not accepting excuses; moving people in and out of the team. The easy life avoids these difficult moments, but leadership is not about the easy life. It is about making a difference.

Conclusion

It is true that leaders need to be skilled but it is not enough. The best leaders need the right mindset. If we call mindset 'habits of mind' then mindset can also be treated as learnable. But leadership is more than just 'know what' skills. It is also 'know how' skills and mindset.

Note

1   J Owen (2015) *Mindset of Success*, Kogan Page, London

MYTH 23

Leadership is about survival of the fittest

To finish first, first you must finish.

There are two myths here:

1 Leaders are the fittest.
2 Becoming a leader is about surviving.

We will explore each myth in turn.

You have to be the fittest to be a leader

At one level, this is tautology. If the person who becomes a leader is the one who best fits the role, then by definition the leader is the fittest person. But that is not the standard version of the myth. The standard version of the myth can be seen in sycophantic profiles of leaders in the business media. There is one group of leaders, normally male, who like to portray themselves as super-fit super heroes; they will usually get up three hours before everyone else wakes up and complete an Ironman triathlon before dashing off to transform their firm.

Why this myth matters

This myth raises an important question: do you need to be fit to lead? Are the demands of modern leadership so intense, with a need to be 'on' 24/7, that only the fittest can survive the leadership marathon?

There is ample evidence you do not need to be an Ironman athlete to lead. Winston Churchill was clearly fit in his youth; he took part in one of the last full cavalry charges in British history.[1] But by the time he became Prime Minister in 1940 he was 66 years old, fat and probably alcoholic and depressive. He was eventually joined in the war effort by President Roosevelt. In 1944 Roosevelt, who suffered from polio, was found to have high blood pressure, atherosclerosis, coronary artery disease causing angina pectoris, and congestive heart failure.[2] Even the super-fit wonder kids of today might find fighting a world war to be quite testing, and yet neither Roosevelt not Churchill were pin-ups for the fitness industry.

But there is one area where fitness does play a part in leadership performance: sleep.

The traditional view of sleep is that it is like lunch: it is for wimps.[3] Young graduates at top investment banks and consulting firms often go through rites of passage where they either pull an all-night session, or at least like to be seen to do an all-night shift by leaving their jackets at their desks.

This is a huge error. The same firms which value the commitment of people working all night would probably fire the same person if they arrived in the morning drunk. But research shows that drinking and lack of sleep have the same effect on performance: reaction times slow down and judgement gets worse.[4] Here are the effects of sleep on the likelihood of having a car crash the next day:

- 6–7 hours' sleep: 1.3 times the crash risk
- 5–6 hours' sleep: 1.9 times the crash risk
- 4–5 hours' sleep: 4.3 times the crash risk
- under 4 hours' sleep: 11 times the crash risk

Don't fool yourself: you cannot achieve peak performance on little sleep.

Lessons for leaders

The good news is that you do not need to be super fit to succeed. But you do need good health and good sleep. You really can sleep your way to the top.

Leadership is about survival

Leaders do not have to be the fittest, but they do have to survive. The world is full of outstanding people who have crashed out, burned out or dropped out. The saying from the sailing world is apt: to finish first, first you must finish. There is no point in going fast and then capsizing. There is a theory that leaders are like tea bags: you only know how good they are when they land up in hot water.[5]

For leaders, the difference between failure and success is as simple as giving up. The tea bag theory suggests that leaders are defined by a few moments of truth which are often crises. Whether or not a leader survives these crises shows you how good they are.

Why this myth matters

All leaders go through dark periods in their careers. These times can be very testing and very lonely. The temptation to seek a quieter life elsewhere can be overwhelming; the dream of the vegan farm in Vermont starts to grow. And if you want to chase that dream, you should. Leadership is an exciting and challenging journey, but it is not for everyone. But if you want to stay on the leadership journey you need to have or build the resilience to take you through hard times as well as good. To paraphrase Nietzsche: 'That which does not break you, makes you stronger.'[6] Crises are not obstacles on the path to leadership. They are the high road to leadership. Embrace them, don't avoid them.

Lessons for leaders

Fortunately, there is a wide body of evidence about how to build resilience and weather the storm of a crisis. Much of the work was done in the most extreme circumstances, from Nazi concentration camps[7] to Vietnamese prisoners of war camps.[8] If you can survive those sorts of conditions, you can probably survive the challenges of leadership.

Here are 10 ways to build your resilience:

1 *Find meaning in what you do.* As a leader, you should make a difference. That is a contribution worth celebrating.

2 *Take control.* The difference between pressure and stress is control. Most people react better to some pressure rather than no pressure. But when there is pressure and you have no control because you depend on other people and events, then stress soars. In practice, you can never control everything you need to control, so find those things you can control in your career and life, and make the most of those.

3 *Stay positive.* Focus on what you can do, and drive to action. There are always plenty of things you cannot do, so there is little point in worrying about them. If there is only one thing you can do, do that.

4 *Be adaptable.* The shortest way between two points may be a straight line, but if you are sailing against the wind then the quickest and only way is a zig zag. This means you always need a plan B for when things go wrong. As Mike Tyson elegantly put it: 'Everyone has a plan until they get punched in the mouth.' What is your plan B?

5 *Find support.* Do not suffer alone.

6 *Count your blessings.* When things are bleak, it is easy to believe that everything is always bleak. Don't talk yourself down. Professionally and personally you will have much you can draw on. Professionally, you still have skills and experience that are valued; personally, we are all lucky to be living free from famine, war and disease for a start.

7 *Use perspective.* Everyone fails on the path to success. Here is basketball legend Michael Jordan: 'I've missed over 9,000 shots in my career. I've lost almost 300 games. Twenty-six times I've been trusted to take the game-winning shot and missed. I've failed over and over and over again in my life. And that is why I succeed.'[9]

8 *Use humour.* The Royal Marines Commandos understand extreme adversity, even in training. They do not talk about surviving adversity. One of their four core values is cheerfulness in the face of adversity: 'How better to endure than with humour? One of the four Commando Spirit characteristics, cheerfulness in the face of adversity, is made possible only by humour, which, although not readily recognized as a quality anywhere else, is actually fundamental [to] the way the Corps operates.'[10] Cheerfulness is the ultimate antidote to adversity.

9 *Embrace adversity.* Resilience is like your credit card: the more you use it, the more you are allowed to use it. As with courage, you can grow your resilience by exposing yourself to situations which test you and stretch you. If you always live life in your comfort zone you will never build the resilience required to sustain yourself in adversity. Push yourself.

10 *Enjoy what you do*, because you only excel at what you enjoy.

Conclusion

These myths are only half true. You do not need to be the fittest to lead, but you do need to be fit and alert. And although you need the persistence to survive, survival simply gets you into a leadership position. Surviving does not mean you are leading. It is a necessary but not sufficient condition of leadership.

Notes

1 Charge of the 21st Lancers in the Battle of Omdurman, 2 September 1898: 400 British cavalry charged 2,500 Mahdist infantry.

2 Wikipedia. Franklin D Roosevelt: Declining health, 2022, https://en.wikipedia.org/wiki/Franklin_D._Roosevelt#Declining_health (archived at https://perma.cc/BUC4-GUCR)

3 'Lunch is for wimps' is one of the classic lines from Gordon Gekko in the 1987 movie *Wall Street*.

4 AAA Foundation for Traffic Safety. Acute sleep deprivation and crash risk, 2016, https://aaafoundation.org/acute-sleep-deprivation-risk-motor-vehicle-crash-involvement/ (archived at https://perma.cc/U3CE-B7UT)

5 I am slightly indebted to Dame Julia Cleverdon for recounting this theory to me. I am hugely indebted to her for all her support to me over the years.

6 F Nietzsche (1889/1895; 1977) *Twilight of the Idols and the Anti-Christ*, trans R J Hollingdale, Penguin, London. The original quotation was: 'From life's school of war: what does not kill me makes me stronger.'

7 Logotherapy was developed by Viktor Frankl after his experiences in a Second World War concentration camp, documented in his 1946 book, *Man's Search for Meaning*, Beacon Press, Boston.

8   The Stockdale paradox is named after Admiral Jim Stockdale, who was held captive for eight years during the Vietnam war. See S Rochester and F Kiley (2007) *Honor Bound: American prisoners of war in Southeast Asia, 1961–1973*, Naval Institute Press, Annapolis

9   R Goldman and S Papson (1998) *Nike Culture: The sign of the swoosh*, Sage, Thousand Oaks, 49

10   Royal Navy. It's a state of mind, find out if you have it, www.royalnavy. mod.uk/careers/royal-marines#:~:text=Unselfishness.,biting% 20cold%20or%20dense%20jungles (archived at https://perma.cc/ 6Z4S-FTWW)

MYTH 24

It's not what you know, it's who you know

Leaders need both talent and networks
on their leadership journey.

Throughout history there have been conspiracy theories which hold that the world is run by shadowy cabals: the Illuminati, Opus Dei and the Freemasons have all been fingered at some point. If an organization is closed, it attracts rumours. A cursory glance at the Freemasons would exclude them as masters of our destiny. If you hang out at a café near their Grand Temple in Holborn, London, you will see large numbers of ageing men dressed like superannuated butlers stopping off for a quick coffee on their way to the Temple. They look like retired civil servants on a day out, rather than grand masters of anything. The conspiracy theorist would just say that proves what good cover they have for their sinister plots made by more senior and secretive Masons. You can never fully disprove a good conspiracy theory.

In business, there is a recurrent theme that jobs go to closed networks. The nature of these networks varies; sometimes it is referred to as the old school tie. If you went to the right school or college, then all the alumni will help each other to the top jobs; for others it is as simple as the all-male club conniving in the toilets to keep women out of top jobs. Others point to the tentacle-like networks of leading firms such as Goldman Sachs and McKinsey which are able to parachute executives into leading roles in business and government.[1] The assumption is that these alumni networks are self-serving; alumni will give business and jobs to their previous employer.

There is some evidence of a network effect. McKinsey alumni provide the CEOs for over 150 firms with a turnover of $1 billion or more. But correlation is not the same as causation. The innocent explanation for the success of McKinsey consultants is that they are all very smart, very driven and have been trained to have good strategy skills. In other words, they are good raw material for becoming a CEO.

PERHAPS IT IS WHO YOU KNOW: ENA AND THE ENARQUES[2]

The École Nationale d'Administration was set up by France to make entry into the highest levels of government more open and more democratic. Entry into ENA is by a fearsome two-part examination, which is open to all. Up to 100 students graduate from ENA every year; it is truly exclusive compared to places like Harvard, Oxford and Cambridge, which admit thousands of students each year. Anyone who graduated from ENA was called an Enarque, and was very bright and very privileged.

Since ENA was set up after the Second World War it has provided 10 presidents or prime ministers of France, 64 ministers or secretaries of state, and the heads of a complete alphabet soup of international organizations: UNESCO, the IMF, ECHR, European Central Bank, EBRD and the European Commission. It has also provided the CEOs for at least 20 of France's leading firms.

In research with the Enarques, it was striking that they all knew each other and how high they graduated in the graduation list. It is genuinely a close-knit community.

The curious result is that although ENA was set up to make entry to the top of French society more open, it has had the perverse effect of making it more closed. If you graduate from ENA you are on the fast track to the top; if you graduate from elsewhere you will have to work even harder to succeed. Perhaps the old school tie really does matter.

In the end, ENA was too successful. In 2021 President Macron, who is an Enarque, announced that he would close ENA and replace it with another Grande Ecole, which is intended to be more open. Time will tell.

Why this myth matters

Leaders need both talent and networks on their leadership journey. It is not a choice between one or the other.

Lessons for leaders

In practice, leaders need both talent and networks. Most of this book focuses on talent and what you need to do to succeed. This section will focus not on what you know, but who you know; building your networks.

Join the power network

If you really believe that the way to the top is through McKinsey, then join McKinsey. That is the point at which you will discover that talent is required to gain admission to the network. Talent and networks go together; what you know and who you know both matter.

If you believe that the Illuminati, Opus Dei or Freemasons are the way to the top, you could join them. But be prepared to be disappointed, unless wearing fancy regalia and following byzantine rituals gives you pleasure.

McKinsey estimate that 450 of their alumni are CEOs of billion dollar firms around the world,[3] including 70 out of the Fortune 500 firms.[4] That is a very powerful network, but it still leaves plenty of room for you to succeed. There are over 2,000 publicly quoted billion dollar firms and many more large private firms, as well as huge organizations in the public and voluntary sectors. McKinsey monopolize perhaps just 1–2 per cent of top CEO positions.

Build your own network

Your network is a powerful route to your next role. Estimates vary, but between 40 and 85 per cent of jobs are found through networking. Even the lower estimate indicates that your personal network is a powerful tool.

Your most important network is in your current firm. Inevitably you will have a network of colleagues and team members who are at or near your level. This is a vital network to help you make things happen, but you also need a network which can steer you to the next opportunity. At a minimum, be nice to HR; they know what opportunities are likely to emerge. This allows you to position yourself appropriately for the opportunity ahead of time; you gain first mover advantage.

You also need one or two powerful sponsors in the firm. These are people at least two levels above you who understand the politics and can shield you; they can help you avoid the Death Star assignments and nudge you to the better opportunities. Senior people always appreciate flattery, always want information about what is really going on, and always need discretionary help on new ideas and challenges. Make yourself useful to them.

Finally, pay attention to your industry network and profile. Conferences are a great way to find out what competitors, suppliers and buyers are thinking and doing. They are also a great way to identify potential personal opportunities, to build your profile and extend your network. Sites like LinkedIn tell the world who you are, but you need to meet people face-to-face to build rapport and trust.

Conclusion

Is it what you know or who you know? You need both as a leader, so this is a semi-myth.

Notes

1 D McDonald (2013) *The Firm: The story of McKinsey and its secret influence on American business*, Simon & Schuster.

2 This is based on original research by the author. A brief summary appeared in Management Today: J Owen, Leadership styles in France and the UK, Management Today, 2007, www.managementtoday.co.uk/leadership-styles-france-uk/article/669368 (archived at https://perma.cc/M4RR-8ZY7)

3 McKinsey. Thirty thousand leaders, 2015, www.mckinsey.com/about-us/new-at-mckinsey-blog/thirty-thousand-leaders (archived at https://perma.cc/8ZNF-N7NE)

4 D Markovits. How McKinsey destroyed the middle class, The Atlantic, 2020, www.theatlantic.com/ideas/archive/2020/02/how-mckinsey-destroyed-middle-class/605878/ (archived at https://perma.cc/VCX4-8YK6)

Power comes from your position

The leader cannot achieve things by relying on formal authority only.

Traditionally, firms were organized on military lines. This made sense, because before the Industrial Revolution the only large-scale organizations were the church and the army. The army seemed to offer better insights into how to organize large numbers of people than the church, so from the start of our industrial age firms copied military models of management. To this day, we hear echoes of this military heritage when firms talk about competitive warfare, fighting battles, holding positions, divisions and officers of the firm.

The military heritage lives on as a command and control hierarchy. Even firms that are becoming flatter still rely on very clear schemes of delegation. Different sorts of authority are attached to different sorts of role. Some people have budget power, others may have approval power. Getting a decision made in a large firm can be a byzantine exercise where you discover many people have the power to say no, and no one wants to take the risk of saying yes. Most corporate approval systems are, in effect, disapproval systems. Success requires avoiding disapproval.

Once people have power, they guard it jealously. The less power they have, the more they protect it. Asking a security guard to use common sense instead of following an insane procedure is an exercise in futility. All they have is their procedure: take that away and you take away their job.

Why this myth matters

The world has changed since the Industrial Revolution, and the nature of the firm has changed as well. Large firms used to be like medieval walled cities: they contained everything they needed to survive. Famously, from 1928 to 1945, the Ford Motor Company even built the Fordlandia and Belterra rubber plantations in Brazil to secure their rubber supplies.[1]

The walls of the firm have come down, and firms have opened up to the world. Firms are specializing more and more in the activities they undertake, which means they become dependent on a complex web of suppliers, partners and customers. Within the firm, the walls between functions and business units are also coming down. Functional silos were the hallmark of command and control firms; the matrix is the hallmark of many firms today.

In this new world, the leader cannot achieve things by relying on formal authority only, because no leader has enough formal authority. In the past, authority and responsibility were matched; now responsibility for a leader is routinely far greater than their authority.

The Industrial Revolution has finally succumbed to a leadership revolution. In the past, leaders made things happen through people they controlled. Now leaders have to make things happen through people they don't control, and that changes everything. It means leaders have to learn the art of leading without formal power. They need a new set of skills around influencing people, decisions and events.

Lessons for leaders

Leaders still derive power from their position, but that is no longer enough. Leaders need to build networks of trust and influence across and beyond the firm, and they have to be able to influence events and decisions.[2]

The topic of influence is too large to cover here, but all leaders should acquire the basic skills of building influence:

1 *Build trust.* Always deliver on your commitments. Find common ground with your colleagues: common interests, needs and priorities. Make it easy for your colleagues: remove risks and obstacles to them working with you.

2 *Create loyal followers.* Show you are genuinely interested in each member of your team and their careers: understand their needs; manage their expectations; build trust by having difficult conversations positively and early; always deliver on your commitments to them.

3 *Focus on outcomes.* Work to clear goals which have visibility and impact across the organization. Find your claim to fame, and then stake your claim; make sure people know about it.

4 *Take control.* Have a clear plan for your department, know what will be different as a result of your work, build the right team, and get the right budget and support for your plan. Do not accept the plan, team and budget you inherit as sacrosanct. You should build a legacy, not just inherit one.

5 *Pick your battles.* Follow Sun Tzu's three rules of warfare: only fight when there is a prize worth fighting for; only fight when you know you will win; only fight when there is no other way of achieving your goal.[3] It is better to win a friend than it is to win an argument.

6 *Manage decisions.* Understand the rational decision (what is the best cost, risk, benefit trade off?), manage the politics (what will the CEO and power brokers expect?) and the emotional decision (what do I feel most confident about and what will my team feel committed to?).

7 *Act the part.* Act like other influential people in your organization: be positive, confident and assertive; act like a peer to senior staff, not like their bag carrier.

8 *Be selectively unreasonable.* Dare to stretch yourself, your team and others; make a difference by going beyond business as usual and beyond the comfort zone. This lets you learn, make an impact and build influence.

9 *Embrace ambiguity.* Crises and uncertainty are wonderful opportunities to make a mark, take control and fill the void of uncertainty and doubt which others create. Ambiguity lets leaders flourish.

10 *Use it or lose it.* Control your destiny or someone else will; you only remain influential if you use your influence.

Conclusion

This myth is misleading and dangerous. Clearly power does come from your position: the president of the United States has more power than a high school janitor in North Dakota. But for most leaders, formal power is not enough. You need to influence and lead people you do not control. Even the president has to persuade and cajole Congress and the public to succeed. This means that 'position comes from power' is true but incomplete and highly misleading: leaders need much more than position.

Notes

1 The Henry Ford. Ford rubber plantations in Brazil, www.thehenryford. org/collections-and-research/digital-resources/popular-topics/brazilian-rubber-plantations/ (archived at https://perma.cc/KAM9-NZT3)
2 The topic of influence is covered at length in J Owen (2012) *How to Influence and Persuade*, Pearson, London
3 Sun Tzu (2009) *The Art of War*, Pax Librorum. Sun Tzu was a Chinese philosopher writing in the 5th century BC.

MYTH 26

Leaders need experience, particularly in management

The hierarchy in many firms resembles a Ponzi scheme.

This myth pits the wisdom and discipline of age against the energy and creativity of youth. It is also perpetuated by the fact that most firms operate as a pyramid. At the top there are a few senior executives who may or may not be leading. At the bottom are myriad workers actually making things happen. In between there are managers of varying seniority. It is no longer necessary to start at the very bottom before you get to the top. The journey from postroom to boardroom is rarely travelled, if only because a lifetime career is becoming as rare as hen's teeth.

The pyramid principle is epitomized by professional services firms which all operate on the basis of grinders, minders and finders. You start with the firm as a young graduate doing hard grunt work, or grinding. If you do that well enough, you may become a minder. Then your job is to manage the work of the grinders, ensuring quality and timely delivery on budget. If you do that well you become an exalted finder; your job is to manage client relationships and bring in the revenues. In other words, the apex of the professional services career is often to become a salesperson, although they always refer to themselves as partners.

Entrenched in the pyramid principle is the idea that you can only become a leader with experience under your belt, and particularly in managing. The logic is that only when you have served your time will you really understand the nature of the business and be able to deliver to clients.

If you look at the classic corporate career, this is reality and not a myth; you have to manage before you can lead.

If you look at any entrepreneur, it clear that it is myth, not reality. Experience isn't everything and you can lead long before you manage. Many of the world's top billionaires had no management experience, but that did not stop them from changing the world and making a fortune. Mark Zuckerberg, Bill Gates and Sergey Brin all lacked any management experience, but successfully set up Facebook, Microsoft and Google. They did not need management experience themselves, because they could hire the best management talent that stock options could buy.

Leadership is not related to your title; you can lead at any level of the firm. Nor do you have to manage before you lead, because leadership and management are different skills. Success at one level does not mean that you will succeed at the next level. In professional services, minding (managing projects) is fundamentally different from finding (managing client relationships and selling work).

Why this myth matters

The myth is a useful way of keeping junior people in their place. The implicit promise is that if you work hard and pay your dues you may eventually be admitted to the club of privilege at the top of the firm. Inevitably, this is a promise which can be kept for the few, not the many. The myth contains four significant dangers.

Loss of leadership talent

If we believe in age over youth, then we exclude the bulk of the population from the leadership talent pool. We also make the fatal mistake of thinking that you only lead when you reach the top of the organization.

The battle between age and experience applies to seniority and to position, but not to leadership. If you want good leaders at the top of the organization, then you need a strong pipeline of leaders lower down. Being a CEO does not make you a leader; having a junior management title does not stop you from leading. You can lead regardless of your age, experience or position. Equally, not all leaders are good managers; they are very different sorts of role. The result is that people who could be very good in leadership roles never get there, because they are not good enough as managers.

Promotion of the wrong people

Not only do some good leaders never get discovered, but not all good managers are good leaders. In professional services, not all minders (managers) can become good finders (sales and client relations). The skills required are simply different.

Confusing experience with learning

There are people in their fifties who have worked for 30 years, but only have one year of experience repeated 30 times. This can be useful in technical experts; a plumber or a surgeon who has repeated a procedure countless times should be good at it. But if leaders really need experience, then that requires that leaders:

- are exposed to a wide variety of experiences, so that they are not repeating the same year of experience 30 times
- learn from their experience – having experience is different to learning from it

Valuing the wrong things: Wrong incentives

The hierarchy in many firms resembles a Ponzi scheme, in which a disproportionate amount of the rewards go to the people at the top of the pyramid. But seniority is not the same as value. Great sales people and traders can generate huge value for the firm. These people are fortunate because their contribution is visible and quantifiable. Other technical experts, in research, logistics, IT or operations are less fortunate. They may also be delivering huge value, but it is harder to isolate individual contributions and to attach a monetary value to them. But the message from the hierarchy is clear: technical skills are valued less than general management skills.

Lessons for leaders

There is a difference between career management and leadership. You have a choice to make between the two.

Career management

This requires that you follow the development steps of most firms. You have to keep on learning new sets of skills at each level. You do not need to lead; you need to manage very well. This is hard work to sustain over decades of a career, and means that survival is success. The people who reach the top are the ones who have the resilience to stay the course and the ability to avoid major career disasters. Taking large risks is rarely good for career survival.

Leadership

Leadership is about taking people where they would not have got by themselves. It means you can be leading from the very start of your career. You may be leading in a smaller area when you start out, but you can still make a difference. By definition, leaders have to take risks and challenge the way things are if they are to take people where they would not have got by themselves. If you have never failed, you have never taken enough risk. By definition, not all risks can succeed. This means that leaders accelerate their careers: they succeed fast or they fail fast. In practice, all leaders are serial failures, but they learn from their experiences and have the resilience to pick themselves up and try again. There is no such thing as 'good enough' for a leader, because improvement is always possible.

It is easy to keep on repeating an exercise and never really learning or improving. Many people learn how to swim adequately and then never improve; they stick with what works for them, even if it is not very good. A leader has to keep on growing and developing.

There is a very simple method of learning from everyday experience. After each key event, which might be a meeting, presentation or conversation, ask yourself two questions: 'What went well?' (WWW) and 'Even better if...?' (EBI).

- *What went well?* Most of us are very poor at learning from success. We learn vividly from the failures of others and ourselves but we take success for granted. But success is not natural or easy. Events are always conspiring to make things worse. Colleagues let us down, competition makes life hard, governments get in the way, key staff leave and random events happen. When something works well, pause for a moment and ask yourself what you did to make that happen. Catch yourself succeeding and then make it a habit. Even when things have gone awry, you may have done something to avert an even greater setback. Asking what went well is not just about making yourself feel good, although that helps. It is about discovering your leadership success formula and then applying it regularly.

- *Even better if...?* Avoid WWW's evil twin: 'What went wrong?' That is a recipe for misery. Ask yourself a more productive question: 'Even better if...?' However well or poorly an event went, there is always something you could do better.

The WWW and EBI habit can be applied in a few seconds as you walk down the corridor; you can use it to review the day or week as you travel back from work. It is also a very good discipline to use with your team to review events of the day. It creates the learning habit and accelerates team and personal improvement.

In reality, it is not a binary choice between leadership and career management. Even the most dedicated career manager will occasionally step up and take the lead; even the most ambitious leader will have to stabilize their career and their firm from time to time. Career managers will experience career as a noun; leaders experience career as a verb. Both choices are legitimate: you choose.

Conclusion

The ability to learn is more important than years spent in role. Unsuccessful leaders do not learn from experience; successful leaders learn most from experience. So you need experience, but you need to learn from it.

The experience does not need to be in management, as shown by successful (and often young) entrepreneurs. The idea that management is necessary to progress to a leadership position is widespread – most firms operate on this basis. But, despite being damaging, the approach is not fatal to firms. They may lose future leaders who are not good managers, but that does not matter. There are enough good managers who can become leaders, which means that firms can have their cake and eat it in terms of leadership and management.

MYTH 27

The first 90 days are make or break

Starting a revolution is risky, and many revolutions eat their own children.

This myth states that the first 90 days in role are the make or break time for a new leader. At the end of the first 90 days (or 100 days, as you wish), everyone will have made their mind up about you. At its simplest it is a call to action. The challenge is that every adviser has a different idea about what action you have to take in those first 90 days. The two extremes can be characterized as:

- Start the revolution.
- Gain acceptance.

Start the revolution

The first 90 days are your honeymoon period where you have the most freedom to act. Opposition to you will not yet have crystalized, and most people will want to make a good impression with the new boss. So this is when you have to act.

The revolution should have two main components:

- *Reorganize.* In theory, reorganizations are about improving the organization. But as you watch the carousel turn from customer focus, to functions, to geography and back again you realize that it is not moving forwards, it is just moving round. But reorganizing helps in two ways, especially for a new manager. First, it is a way of gaining control. Once you have fired or moved aside a few people and promoted people you trust, you have the team you want and you have shown that you are prepared to use your power. Troublemakers will think twice about making trouble. Second, you send a message to the organization about what is going to be important. That message should back up the second part of the revolution: a new strategy or vision.

- *A new vision or strategy.* The idea of the first 90 days is that the longer you leave things as they are, the harder they are to change. In the first 90 days, people are expecting change, so this is your golden opportunity to set a new direction. This works if you already understand enough about the team or the firm, but if you are simply working on instinct and past experience, it carries the obvious danger that you might be wrong. What worked in the past in a different context is not guaranteed to work today in a new context. Sometimes it pays to prepare.

Gain acceptance

This more modest version of the first 90 days is about embedding yourself into the firm and laying the foundations for future success. The three main components of this are:

- Meeting all the key stakeholders inside and outside the firm, and understanding their motivations and agendas.
- Meeting regular staff and customers to get a better feel of what is really happening in the operations and market place of the firm.
- Reviewing and thoroughly understanding the strategy, finances and capabilities of the firm: people, technology and operations.

There is good reason to follow the more modest 90-day agenda. Starting a revolution is risky, and many revolutions eat their own children. Your revolution may lead to the Promised Land, or it may lead to the desert. Or it may simply fail to take off if you have not understood the politics and power properly. This means it makes sense to prepare for the revolution before launching it.

You can unite the two extreme approaches to the first 90 days. Here is how: spend the first 89 days gaining acceptance, understanding the business and laying the foundations for your revolution. Launch your revolution on day 90, when you are confident of success.

Why this myth matters

Clearly the first 90 days are important. But that is like saying leadership is important: it gives us no clue about what we should be doing.

In practice, many new leaders find themselves swamped. There is a deluge of day-to-day noise to deal with: crises, routine administration, emails, meetings, reviews and reports. Even finding out who is who and how the expenses system works takes time and diverts effort. And that is the real message of the first 90 days myth: don't let yourself drown in the noise of the day-to-day. You have to rise above the noise and develop a clear path forward. If you are only dealing with the noise then you will be managing but you will not be leading. You will not be taking people where they would not have got by themselves.

The message from this myth is clear: rise above the noise. Avoid getting caught in the swamp of the day-to-day and build your vision for the future.

Lessons for leaders

Here are three alternative perspectives on the first 90 days challenge.

The first 90 days, or the previous 90 days?

Generals believe that most battles are won or lost before the first shot is fired. One side is better prepared, with more resources, and is in the right position. The same is true of new leaders: your fate may be sealed before you arrive.

This means you have to ensure you are set up for success before you take up your new role. Before you agree to a new role, your bargaining power is at maximum. Once you have accepted your new role, all your bargaining power evaporates. The previous 90 days are vital, and some of the keys to success include asking:

- Is this a firm which is going to succeed? Success is far easier in a growing firm than one which is retrenching. Is the firm in a growing market with a good competitive position? Do your homework.
- Does the role suit me? Is this the sort of challenge I can address, and is it the sort of culture in which I can thrive? Does the firm have the sorts of values I am comfortable with?
- Will I have the right resources? What are the capabilities of the team? Will I have sufficient budget? Will I have any sponsors who can help me and support me?

The first 90 days or the first 90 milliseconds?

First impressions matter. Research shows that we draw inferences about people after less than one second.[1] The same research shows that we become more confident about our impressions the longer we are exposed to someone, although confirmation bias means we tend to reinforce our first impression.

Leaders can put this to their advantage. If people judge you by how you look and behave, then project the image you want them to see. Leadership is, in many ways, live performance art in which you act out the best of who you are. That takes continued practice and constant effort.

Make sure you act the part you want to be.

Back to basics: The art of taking control

As a leader, you have to take control. You know you are in control when the following three conditions are in place:

- *Idea*. You need a clear idea of how you will make a difference. This is your vision or strategy. Are you pushing your agenda, or simply following the agenda you inherited, with a couple of tweaks?

- *People*. You need the right team to deliver your idea. The team you inherited may or may not be the right one for the future. You also need the right network of support across and beyond the firm.

- *Money*. Any vision needs budget. Ideally, make sure you have this before you accept the role. The longer you stay in role the more you will be implied to have accepted the budget, agenda and team you inherited.

The first 90 days clearly matter for a leader. But for a good leader, every day matters and every minute matters.

Conclusion

There is nothing magical about the first 90 days. Of course the first 90 days matter, but every day and every minute and the 90 days before you take up post also matter. So that nudges the first 90 days back into the land of myth, or more accurately into the land of a nice money-earning fad for gurus, coaches and advisers.

Note

1   J Willis and A Todorov. First impressions: Making up your mind after a 100 ms exposure to a face, *Psychological Science*, 2006, 17, 592–98

You can teach leadership

Leadership cannot be taught, but you can learn it.

If we can all learn to lead, then it should be possible to teach people how to lead. There are endless leadership courses and books which claim to be able to teach you how to lead. The fact that people offer these courses and people buy them indicates that people believe leadership can be taught. So, at first glance, teaching leadership appears to be reality, not myth.

But we should pause before writing off the myth.

It is clear that you cannot read a book on leadership and become a leader by page 259. Equally, the two-day leadership course will not turn you instantly into a leader. If you can be taught leadership, it is neither easy nor instant.

As an exercise, I ask groups how they have learned to lead. I let them choose two main ways of learning from six sources. You might try the exercise as well. Choose which two of the following have been most important for you in learning about leadership:

- books
- courses
- peers (inside and outside work)
- role models (inside and outside work)
- bosses (good and bad lessons)
- personal experience

Virtually no one chooses books or courses. That could be bad news for an author who runs courses on leadership. Everyone chooses some combination of personal and observed experience. This makes perfect sense. We see someone do something well, and we try to copy it. We see another person implode spectacularly and we make a note not to repeat that particular mistake. We see what works in practice and in our context. We create our own unique formula for success, based on how we work and where we work.

The problem with discovering leadership this way is that it is a random walk: bump into good bosses and experiences and you accelerate your career. Poor bosses and experiences lead you straight into a dead end. You have to convert your random walk of experience into a structured journey of discovery. This is where books and courses can help: they help you make sense of the nonsense you encounter and to structure your journey of success.

Why this myth matters

This myth matters for two reasons, because it shows:

- how organizations should develop leaders
- why most leadership training is doomed to fail

How organizations should develop leaders

The best leadership organizations build their leadership programmes around how people actually learn: from experience. That means they will structure your leadership journey for you. The Royal Marines Commandos put aspiring officers through a gruelling 18-month training programme; the best firms put new graduates through a series of experiences as well as training to develop them.

Inevitably, the best firms also select rigorously, but they are all selecting on different criteria. What it takes to succeed in the Royal Marines, the Civil Service, investment banking or the creative arts, for example, are completely different: attitudes to risk, courage, compliance and creativity are different in each. Although they select on different criteria, they all recognize that managing the leadership journey involves developing and testing people with a range of relevant experiences.

Why most leadership training is doomed to fail

Look back at the list of sources of learning about leadership: very few people claim to have learned about leadership from training courses. The symptom of this is the frequency with which people find themselves unable to attend a training course (unless it is in a nice location) and the frequency with which training is one of the first items to be cut in the annual budget squeeze. There are three reasons why leadership training is not valued:

- Going on any form of leadership training is often perceived as a sign of weakness. Going on a course to learn a technical skill such as IT, or finance is not weak. Going on a course to learn about motivating people implies that you are no good at motivating people.
- Leadership courses are generic solutions to specific challenges. The skills you need and how you deploy them depend on your context. Working out how to adapt universal lessons to your needs is hard in theory and even harder in practice.
- There is a time lag between learning and doing. Managers rightly want learning which helps them now; they need to try new ideas while they are still fresh in the mind. The half life of any learning is very short, unless it is constantly tested and put into practice.

None of these challenges are about the quality of the course. Some courses are excellent, others less so. These are all structural challenges which are inherent to the nature of all formal courses. The best programmes attempt to address these challenges, but it is as thankless as pushing water uphill.

Lessons for leaders

Leadership cannot be taught, but you can learn it. This is because your path to leadership is a journey of discovery. You have to discover what works for you in your context: there is no universal formula for success. And as your context will keep on changing, you must keep on learning throughout your career. The people who stop learning are the ones who get marooned in their career.

Ultimately, the only person who can navigate the leadership journey is you. You have to make sure that you get the right experiences, projects, assignments and bosses to build your career.

Your challenge is to make sure that your journey is not a random walk, and that you do not get lost in all the noise and nonsense you encounter day-to-day. That is where books and courses come in: they can help you step back and see more clearly where you need to go and what you need to do. Hopefully this book is your map: it shows you what your options are, where some of the pitfalls are and lets you decide where you want to go on your leadership journey.

Conclusion

You cannot read a textbook and become a leader. But you can learn to lead, and firms can structure experiences and support to help you learn. So this is a confusing myth – you cannot be taught leadership but you can learn it.

MYTH 29

Leaders know when to move on

Leaders live in a gilded cage where few people dare to challenge them, and many people choose to flatter them.

Most firms pay attention to succession planning. Firms need a pipeline of talent at all levels to provide the leaders of the future, and to provide cover for the present. A deep reservoir of talent is insurance against losing key executives unexpectedly.

Leaders pay lip service to the idea of succession planning. They know it is good for the firm; they are less enamoured of the idea that they should make themselves redundant. What is good for the firm is not always so good for the individual.

If you really want to both annoy and scare a CEO, ask what they are going to do when they retire. To many CEOs, retirement is a sort of living death. As CEO, they are used to being a master of the universe; the world revolves around them and they have a clear sense of purpose and relevance. They may work hard, but the work gives structure to their lives, and the firm creates a society for them. When they retire, they lose everything: they lose the structure of the day, the society of the firm, the purpose and meaning of work and they are no longer the centre of the world.

Logically, leaders may see the need for succession planning. Emotionally, they want to avoid it for as long as possible. To avoid the fate of retirement death they often seek a halfway house where they can pontificate on committees, commissions and charity boards. This is often referred to dismissively as 'going reactive': you are no longer pushing your agenda, but reacting to those of others.

Leaders are right to be suspicious of downshifting. Evidence shows that retirement is bad for your health. A report published by the London-based Institute of Economic Affairs found that retirement increased the chances of suffering from depression by 40 per cent, while it increased the probability of having at least one diagnosed physical ailment by about 60 per cent.[1] There is a familiar pattern. In the first year of retirement, health improves as the stress of the job is removed; new-found freedom is used to fulfil life dreams such as travel. This keeps the retiree occupied. But then health deteriorates. The impact of losing the social and daily structure of work hits home. Watching television aimlessly from day to day is not great for health. Depression and a serious ailment normally strike within six years of retirement.[2]

Finally, leaders want to stay in post because they start to believe they really are indispensable to the fate of the firm.

Leaders live in a gilded cage where few people dare to challenge them, and many people choose to flatter them. If things go well, that proves to the leader that they are doing a great job. When things go wrong, it is even stronger proof that the boss is indispensable: setbacks are clear evidence that the rest of the team are not up to their current jobs, let alone the top job.

Quietly, many leaders are happy with poor succession. If the firm struggles after the CEO departs, that is proof positive (at least to the departed CEO) that they really were the key to success, and that no one else could possibly emulate them. In reality, a failure of the new CEO is the failure of the old CEO in not securing the succession properly.

Why this myth matters

It is very hard to get rid of a CEO, especially in countries where the governance allows for the concentration of powers in the hands of the CEO. When the CEO is also the president and chair of the board, you have a real problem. There is no one to challenge the CEO, especially as they are able to fill the board with friends and allies. These friends are often other CEOs or chairs who all appoint each other to each other's boards. They create a CEO self-preservation society which is good for them, not for the firm.

Even with proper governance in place, most boards are deeply risk averse. Dumping a CEO and finding a new one is the riskiest thing a board can do, and it causes a lot of work. Non-executives have limited appetite for work or risk. This means that they will only move when there is a real crisis and when the CEO is obviously failing: that is too late.

Lessons for leaders

Here are five things you can do to deal with the problem of moving on. All good actors and actresses know how to time their entrances and their exits. Leaders need to do the same.

Visit a graveyard

It is full of executives who thought they were indispensable. Earlier ages were more robust about death than we are. Memento mori were paintings or artefacts which sent out a simple message: 'Remember you must die.' They were popular all the way from the Middle Ages to the Victorian era. They are reminders of how precious and fleeting life is: we have to make the most of every moment.

Prepare for your next move

Leadership is a journey, even when you are the CEO. Work out how you will either sustain or replace what you value about what you do currently: the social network, the structure to the day, the sense of meaning and purpose. These things are far more valuable than your next long-term bonus payment. If you are a CEO you probably have enough money to pay the rent. But money cannot buy you the things that become increasingly important: networks, structure and meaning. These things cannot be developed overnight. You need to start building them at least a few years ahead.

Pay attention to governance

Most CEOs regard the non-executive board as a nuisance: they are a necessary evil which has to be managed. But the governance structure is there for good reason. It is a vital check and balance for the firm and its shareholders. It should be the source of constructive challenge for the CEO. A weak board makes for an easy life for the CEO; a strong board can help deliver strong performance. The CEO should prefer performance to an easy life.

Set yourself term limits

Death concentrates the mind, so does retirement or the prospect of moving on to another role. If you know you have a 'sell by' date stamped on your forehead, then that forces you to think about how you will make a difference in the time available. It creates a sense of urgency and purpose, and does not allow you to drift on endlessly. The US presidency was informally subject to the two-term rule from the time of George Washington, and this was formally acknowledged in the 22nd amendment to the constitution after Franklin D Roosevelt's long stint as president. The contrast with nations where dictators and demagogues cling on to power for life shows the wisdom of clear term limits.

Plan your succession

When Isaac Newton was being acclaimed for his achievements, he modestly replied: 'If I have seen further, it is by standing on the shoulders of giants.'[3] He knew that his success was built on the work of all the scientists who preceded him. This is your opportunity to be the giant on whose shoulders the next leader can stand, and perhaps achieve even greater things. The success of your successor is also your success. Help them on the path to greatness.

Conclusion

This myth is both pervasive and dangerous. It is pervasive because leaders do not know when to move on: they normally have to be nudged or kicked. And it is dangerous because leaders who stay too long damage the firm and ultimately themselves by not knowing what they will do next.

Notes

1 G H Sahlgren (2013) *Work Longer, Live Healthier*, IEA discussion paper no 46, Institute of Economic Affairs, https://iea.org.uk/wp-content/uploads/2016/07/Work%20Longer,%20Live_Healthier.pdf (archived at https://perma.cc/AJA3-KQSN)

2 Kseeker. Can retirement kill you? Defence Forum India, 2013, http://defenceforumindia.com/forum/threads/can-retirement-kill-you.57285/ (archived at https://perma.cc/5ZBC-B8DA)

3 Wikiquote. Sir Isaac Newton, nd, https://en.wikiquote.org/wiki/Isaac_Newton (archived at https://perma.cc/7XA7-ANAZ)

MYTH 30

It's tough at the top

If you want to discover real stress,
do not go to the top of the firm: go to the middle.

How many leaders say it is easy at the top? Probably as many as the number of work–life balance gurus who advise more work. And if it is so tough at the top, why does everyone want to get there?

If we believe that it is easy at the top, then it destroys a large part of the leadership myth. There would be no need to pay leaders large sums of money for doing something easy and enjoyable. The idea of the leader as a hero would bite the dust.

Leaders are happy to live with the idea that it is tough at the top, even if the evidence points in the opposite direction. There are three main elements to the myth:

1 It is stressful at the top.
2 It is hard work at the top.
3 Unique skills are needed at the top.

As ever, this makes the assumption that the person at the top is actually leading. Many people at the top fail the leadership test of taking people where they would not have got by themselves.

It is time to put each part of this myth to the test.

Why this myth matters

'It's tough at the top' is at the heart of leadership mythology. Here is what the evidence shows about each part of the myth.

It is stressful at the top

If you want to discover real stress, do not go to the top of the firm: go to the middle. This is the paranoia zone where stress is at its greatest. The two great drivers of stress are control and ambiguity. People often raise their performance when under pressure, as long as they know what they have to do and they are in control of events. If there is the same pressure to perform but you face ambiguous or contradictory goals, stress levels soar: it is not clear where you should invest your time and effort. If you then also lose control over the outcome, stress levels hit the red zone. Losing control is routine if you depend on colleagues or suppliers to deliver part of your outcome, or to give you permission, or to supply information or resources. Suddenly, you are dependent.

Now look at how ambiguity and control change at different levels of the firm. When you start out, you typically have low control but low ambiguity. It is very clear what you have to do. It may be dull and it may be hard work, but at least it is clear what you need to do to succeed. At the top of the firm, the equation is reversed. You have very high control as the CEO: you are the master of your own destiny. You also have very high ambiguity: there are myriad ways of achieving your goals. Your high level of control effectively converts ambiguity into freedom to act as you wish. Stress should be low.

Leaders in the middle do not get the best of both worlds. They get the worst of ambiguity and control. Leaders in the middle face competing priorities from across the firm. They also have to compete to ensure their own priorities get the support and resources they need. The middle is where ambiguity is high and control is low: it is the real stress zone of the firm.

Leadership is hard work

At one level, leadership is hard work. But at the top, leaders can choose to make it as hard as they want. Ronald Reagan was one of the more successful US presidents: he saw the demise of the Soviet Union and end of the Cold War, he introduced Reaganomics to the world, and negotiated a breakthrough treaty to eliminate an entire class of nuclear weapons. That is not bad for someone who was regarded as lazy: he was reputed to be in his pyjamas watching TV with a TV dinner by 8pm every evening.

Business leaders may want to boast about their achievements, but few will match those of Reagan, however hard they work. They could learn from Reagan's approach to leadership:

1 He knew what he wanted to achieve and focused clearly on that.

2 He knew what he was good at, and focused his energies on that; for all his faults, he was seen as the great communicator. He used that talent to pull the nation and Congress behind him.

3 He was excellent at delegating. At the time the business buzzword was MBWA: management by walking around. He practised an alternative version of MBWA: management by walking away. He trusted his team to do the heavy lifting for him.

You need unique skills at the top

This is true, but irrelevant. You need unique skills in any role. The real question is whether leadership skills are in abundant or limited supply. There appears to be no shortage of talent seeking the top jobs.

Lessons for leaders

One of my professors at university decided to give me some unsolicited career advice: 'Don't join a firm as a junior. Always join as a partner.' The professor correctly understood that life is far better at the top of the firm than at the bottom or the middle. It was, of course, completely useless advice: how do you join at the top, unless you set up your own business?

Leaders at the top can follow Reagan's example if they want to be more effective and work less:

1 Focus on the big issues where you will make a difference.
2 Focus on doing what you do best.
3 Delegate everything else.

Following in Reagan's footsteps, one of the best bosses I ever had was also one of the idlest. He did three things very well:

1 He built trust with senior clients who would open their wallets for him.
2 He negotiated smart budgets. He worked on the basis that it is better to work hard for one month a year negotiating a good budget than to work hard for 11 months being macho trying to chase a 'challenging' budget.
3 He delegated everything else, which meant that teams loved him. His delegation showed that he trusted them, and they responded by performing for him.

These are options which are more easily available at the top of the firm than in the middle. The middle is where it is hardest work. In practice, leaders at the top prefer the hard work, as it reinforces their sense of purpose and importance. But that does not make you a good leader.

Conclusion

It is hard to have sympathy with leaders who complain that it is tough at the top. Everyone has a tough life, and leaders live a gilded life compared to most. Leaders choose to lead and they are fortunate compared with most people. Leaders should enjoy what they do, not complain about it.

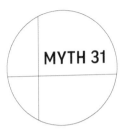

MYTH 31

The buck stops here

Sharing the credit is a good way of claiming the credit.

President Truman kept a sign on his desk saying 'The Buck Stops Here'. It is a sign which has been copied many times and used on many desks elsewhere, at least in the era when leaders still had a desk to call their own.

The sign strikes at the heart of two leadership ideas which are frequently confused: accountability and responsibility. The essential difference between the two is that only one person can be accountable, but many people can share responsibility. From the leader's point of view, that means you can never delegate your accountability, but you must delegate as much responsibility as you can. When you delegate responsibility, you ask someone else to do the task: that is the essence of both leadership and management. Nevertheless, you remain accountable for the outcome of that task, however well or poorly it was done.

Why this myth matters

The myth matters because it is frequently misunderstood or misused. Two examples will make the point.

The accountability trap

All leaders, and managers, sign up to the idea that they are accountable, until the moment they are held to account. It is human nature to want to be accountable for the good stuff, but not for the bad. Even CEOs fall into the accountability trap. Reading an annual report when times are good is to discover that the firm is led by people who have improved the fortunes of the firm through their dedication and brilliance. When results are not so good, we get to discover the role of outrageous fortune in sabotaging the work of the CEO: government has, or has not, intervened; the market has been soft so those pesky customers have not been buying enough at the right price; the weather conspired against us; sneaky competition did things which were clearly unfair. But, whatever happened, it was not the fault of the CEO, who still deserves an outsized bonus.

The responsibility trap

It is a small step from believing that the buck stops here to believing in the hero leader who knows it all and does it all. It is a step which many leaders and their teams are happy to take.

A leader who believes the buck stops here is often unwilling to delegate. They may delegate the routine rubbish, and they may delegate the blame when things go wrong. That is a parody of delegation. But they are often most unwilling to delegate the most challenging tasks. The leader turns to the only person they trust on such challenging tasks: themselves. The greater the challenge, the greater the need for the whole team to rise to the challenge.

Many teams are happy with letting the buck stop with the leader. This gives them the chance to delegate responsibility for the toughest decisions and challenges upwards. By delegating decisions upwards, the team can no longer be held responsible if the decision is the wrong one. Delegating upwards is a safe and lazy way of being a team member. Leaders need to push back: trust the team and challenge them to take responsibility.

Lessons for leaders

Be accountable for good times and bad times

The best leaders take an unexpected approach to accountability in good times and bad.

In good times, the best leaders do not hog all the glory. They are generous in sharing the praise. This has several positive effects. First, it builds huge goodwill among the people who share the glory: most people feel under-recognized, so a little recognition goes a long way. Second, it reinforces the role of the leader: only the person who was at the heart of the success knows who to praise. In effect, sharing the credit is a good way of claiming the credit.

In bad times, the most effective leaders take accountability to heart. They take the blame. This has a transformative effect. It means that the team can move on from finger-pointing and passing the buck. Instead of playing politics and analysing the past, they can look to the future and work out how to solve the problem. It also creates an atmosphere which is positive, productive and trusting. As a leader, you do not want to be making excuses: you want results. Accepting the blame means you move past the excuses stage and onto action and results.

You are accountable for your own feelings

This is perhaps the hardest accountability lesson of all. Imagine you have had a long, hard and frustrating day; you have been running hard to stand still while everything seems to conspire against you. And then someone comes along and decides to wind you up. They know exactly which buttons to press to get a reaction. At this point, you have every right to feel angry, annoyed and upset. But there is no law that says you must feel angry, annoyed and upset: that is your decision.

Knowing that you are accountable for your own feelings is daunting and liberating. Once you know you can choose how you feel, you are no longer at the mercy of external events dictating your mood. It is also a vital leadership technique. You will not be remembered for beating this year's budget by 6.4 per cent: you will be remembered for how you are. In particular, you will be remembered for how you behave at moments of truth, crisis and uncertainty. You can only project a positive and professional face to the world if that is how you feel inside. However you choose to feel, choose well.

You cannot share accountability, but you must share responsibility

This is where President Truman's sign rings true: the buck does stop with the leader. You can delegate everything except your accountability. Ultimately, you are accountable for the outcome. If you delegated responsibility to someone who did not deliver, you are still accountable for that: you chose to delegate, and you have to live with the result of that decision.

In contrast to accountability, effective leaders have to delegate responsibility. You cannot do it all yourself, however brilliant and heroic you may be. If you find it hard to delegate, that is a sign that you do not trust your team. That means there is something wrong either with you or with your team. A key task of any leader is to build the right team (see Myth 14). You will know you have the right team when you are confident about delegating the most challenging roles to them.

Conclusion

This myth is a reality. But the nature of 'the buck stops here' is easily misunderstood. It does not mean micromanaging: it means sharing responsibility, sharing success and being accountable for yourself, your career and your feelings.

MYTH 32

It's lonely at the top

Power creates distance.

At first glance, this myth is... a myth. Look at the diary of most leaders and it will be jam-packed with meetings all day, and the average working day of a leader is often long. The real problem for leaders appears to be that they are not lonely enough; they do not have enough quiet time where they can think and review.

The literature on leadership is split between the hyper-active doers who trumpet their ability to work 100 hours a week, and the hyper-deep thinkers who trumpet how much time they spend thinking. Warren Buffett, the legend-ary investor, is reputed to spend 80 per cent of his time reading or thinking.[1] But Buffett is an outlier in more or less every way. As a fund manager, he needs to spend time thinking, reading and analysing: that is his job. Among leaders, the doers heavily outnumber the thinkers. Leaders like to be seen as dynamic and active, and so that is how they act and how they manage their diaries.

But look again, and you find that this myth may not be a myth at all. It accurately reflects the experience of most leaders. How can leaders be lonely when they are meeting people all day?

Here is how loneliness comes about. As a middle manager, you are used to having your ideas challenged: bosses will tell you what they think about your performance; your failings will be noted. But when you reach the top everything changes:

- Everyone laughs at your jokes, which they ignored before.
- Your half-baked idea is no longer trashed; instead you find someone has gone away and worked it into a proposal.
- You find all sorts of things happening in the firm because that is what you wanted, even when you have not expressed a view on the topic.
- Everyone comes to you with an idea, and they all want a slice of your time, your support and your budget.
- Every project you start is deemed to have succeeded, even when it has failed.

Why this myth matters

At the heart of the problem is power. Power creates distance, and it is distance which creates a sense of loneliness for the leader. Ultimately, the leader starts to doubt if there is anyone they can trust. The lack of trust takes two forms.

Can I trust anyone to tell me the truth?

The more reflective leaders realize that they are being told what they want to hear. They know that when they were on the way up, they learned loyalty: don't give the boss bad medicine and support the boss at all times. But loyalty comes at the price of honesty, and this is why so many leaders value the art of management by walking around. They want to hear and see for themselves what is really happening in the market, or in operations and elsewhere. They trust their own eyes more than they trust the reports that land on their desk. They take to heart the message from John Le Carré: 'A desk is a dangerous place from which to view the world.'[2] That is as true of leaders as it is of spies.

Can I trust anyone with vital decisions?

Some leaders take the reactions of their team at face value. They start to believe that they are genuinely witty and that the team now depends on their unique brilliance and insight. This is how power corrupts. The leader starts to believe that they are indispensable. They take all the key decisions themselves, and when things go wrong blame their team for poor implementation. This is standard operating practice for dictators around the world. Moving from being a leader to a dictator means everyone suffers except for the dictator and a few lucky cronies.

When you find there is no one you can trust, you start to feel very lonely.

Lessons for leaders

The more powerful you are as a leader, the more everyone wants a piece of you: they want your time, support and resources. This means that they will flatter you, support you and praise you. You will find fewer and fewer people who challenge you or criticize you to your face.

Stay objective

You need to discover the truth, however awkward it may be. Talk to customers, suppliers, competitors and staff; bypass the formal channels of communication. Inside the firm, recognize flattery for what it is: flattery. Focus on what is being said, not how it is being said. Given that leaders receive little challenge or feedback, you have to be your own fiercest critic. Constantly challenge and test yourself and your assumptions.

Listen more, talk less

A famous slogan in the Second World War warned people about the danger of spies: 'Idle talk costs lives'. Leaders soon learn that idle talk is very expensive: your throwaway remark will be taken as approval or disapproval for an idea, and action will be taken as a result. It is no use later saying, 'What I really meant was...'. The damage will have been done. The best leaders have two ears and one mouth, and they use them in that proportion: they listen at least twice as much as they talk. Observe leaders in meetings and the most effective ones will say little, but they will ask smart questions at the right moment. Only if you ask the right question can the team provide the right answer.

Trust your team

Asking questions is a good way of delegating; providing answers is a good way of assuming responsibility personally. As a leader, you do not have to prove your heroism by doing everything yourself. You will be judged by what your team achieves, not by who does it. Even if you do not trust your team to tell you the whole truth all the time, you have to trust them to make decisions and to take action. If you try to be the hero, you will be overwhelmed.

Find someone to keep you honest

Julius Caesar, on his triumphal march, had an auriga (slave) constantly repeating 'Memento homo': remember you are human. As a leader, you will not have a slave, but you need someone to challenge, criticize and support you personally. You have to trust them to tell you the truth if you are to stay on top of your game, or raise your game. Without challenge, you will make poor decisions. Without challenge, you will only find out the truth about your performance when your chairman very elegantly slips the knife between your shoulder blades. Your truth teller could be a coach or spouse; it could be a staff person nearing retirement who has nothing to fear, nothing to gain and nothing to lose from telling you the truth. Find someone you can trust with the truth.

Conclusion

At a literal level, it is obvious that leaders are never lonely. But the myth turns out to be true at a psychological level: the leader has few people they can turn to and trust completely. Power is lonely and dangerous.

Notes

1 Thinking or doing? A good example of the trade-off is here: B Scudamore. Why successful people spend 10 hours a week just thinking, Inc., nd, www.inc.com/empact/why-successful-people-spend-10-hours-a-week-just-thinking.html (archived at https://perma.cc/T6NP-CW2P)

2 J Le Carré (1977) *The Honourable Schoolboy*, Hodder and Stoughton, London

The leader makes a difference

Activity is not the same as achievement.

This myth is potentially a tautology. If leaders take people where they would not have got by themselves, then if you are not making a difference you are not leading. Instead, we will relax the definition of leadership and define the leader as the boss. So, does the boss make a difference?

Subjectively, it is obvious that all bosses make some sort of difference, for better or for worse. A good boss will energize the team and a bad boss will demotivate them. But the leadership test of 'making a difference' is tougher than the effect you have on your team. The test is whether you have changed the future for the team and taken them where they would not have got by themselves.

Against this tougher benchmark, many leaders would argue that they are making a difference. Every firm will point to the initiatives they are taking to build market share, open new markets, cut costs, attract and retain customers, simplify their operations and strengthen their talent pool. Firms are a coruscating whirl of activity and change. This activity and change is what leaders are leading, so the evidence points to them making a difference.

Why this myth matters

The Great Man theory of leadership (discussed in Myth 3) goes too far and is largely discredited. Very few leaders can actually change the course of events by sheer willpower. They cannot make this much of a difference. But if leaders are not making some kind of a difference to the destiny of their team, they may as well pack their bags and go home. However, this myth contains two bear traps for leaders.

The myth of the stable baseline

This myth is a killer in business. All your work on improving the business often has little positive effect, for two reasons:

1 *Corporate entropy.* Everything inexorably slides towards chaos. Experienced staff leave and are replaced by more junior staff; customer requirements change; regulations change but never get lighter; the tax man always wants another cut; suppliers let you down and random acts cause crises even before the competition attempts to wreck

your day. In this world, simply maintaining the current level of performance is hard work.

2   *Competition*, which is the curse of capitalism. The benefits of every initiative you take are likely to be competed away to the ultimate benefit of your customers, who are the only winners in the corporate race called betterfastercheaper. If you cut costs by 10 per cent, then the chances are your competitors will cut them as fast. Unless you are in an oligopoly, the cost cuts will not show up in your bottom line, but in prices to your customers. Your leadership team may be brilliant, creative and diligent, but the chances are that the leadership teams of your competitors are equally brilliant, creative and diligent. It is hard to outrun them.

Competition and entropy mean that many leaders find themselves following the advice of the Red Queen in Lewis Carroll's *Through the Looking Glass*: 'If you want to get somewhere else, you must run at least twice as fast as that!'[1] As we shall see, that is the second bear trap for leaders.

Activity is not the same as achievement

The standard response to the problem of the declining baseline is to work harder and do more. How many managers complain that there are not enough initiatives in the firm? We know that in most firms, people are working hard and introducing lots of new initiatives. But few of them actually change the future. We noted in Myth 3 that more than half the firms in the Fortune 500 disappear within a generation. These are not firms led by idiots; they are led by people like you or me.

In practice, most firms are prisoners of their past. They suffer inertia, which makes it hard to change direction when they need to. In most firms the best predictor of next year's budget is this year's budget; the best predictor of next year's strategy is this year's strategy. Of course, the budget and strategy will move over time and each minor change will be the result of major discussion. But the despite all the activity of the leadership, the destiny of the firm rarely changes.

That is not an indictment of leadership; it is a reflection of just how hard it is to maintain a stable baseline. If leaders really want to make a difference, they have to do more than run faster. They need to change the rules of engagement: buy a bicycle instead of running.

Lessons for leaders

If you are to make a difference as a leader, you have to beat the challenge of the declining baseline. This is a tough challenge which few leaders can achieve consistently.

Leaders operate at three levels:

1 *Maintaining performance*. This deals with the day-to-day noise of organizational life. It is hard work because of corporate entropy: you have to stop the slow slide towards chaos. Every day brings new challenges. The battle against the declining baseline never stops. This supervisory work is necessary but not enough.
2 *Improving performance*. This is where leaders launch endless initiatives which ultimately get competed away to the benefit of competition. This is classic managerial work: find ways of improving what already exists. It is

hard work but essentially safe work. You are dealing with existing systems and ways of working.

3 *Changing performance.* This is not about improving performance or seeking excellence. It is about daring to rethink what you do and how you do it. Create new rules of the game. Stop running faster and faster and either change direction or buy that bicycle. This may sound exciting and inspirational, but the reality is different. It is highly risky because you have to challenge how things are done today. That makes it hard work, because you will encounter widespread political resistance to anything that makes deep change, rather than simply improving on existing ways. It is the fast track to success, or failure.

If you aspire to lead, you have to make a difference. But making a difference in a way that changes the future is exceptionally hard. You have to beat the challenges of competition, corporate entropy and the declining baseline. If you can do all that, you know you are a leader.

Conclusion

Leaders are often confused about what makes a difference and whether they are making a difference. 'Making a differ-ence' is much claimed but little achieved, which takes it firmly out of the realms of reality and into the realms of fantasy. Leaders claim to make a difference more than they do.

Note

1 L Carroll (1872) *Through the Looking-Glass*, Macmillan, London.

MYTH 34

Money matters for leadership

Senior executives show that they are very good at rent seeking, but fail to prove any link between the rents they extract and the performance they deliver.

Sherlock Holmes drew the attention of the police officer to 'the curious incident of the dog in the night-time'. The officer protested that the dog did nothing in the night-time. 'That was the curious incident,' replied Holmes.[1]

Occasionally, what we do not hear or see is as important as what we can hear and see. But, as Holmes' story shows, it is very hard to notice what is not there. So what is missing from theories of leadership?

The glaring omission is money. No one talks about money. At grand dinner parties, money, along with sex, death and religion, is normally avoided as being too controversial a subject. There is certainly much that could be written about sex and leadership, but we will focus on money. Is money too grubby for leadership experts?

Money matters for leadership for two reasons:

1 If you want to lead, normally you need money.
2 Many leaders earn great wealth. This raises a basic question which remains unanswered: what motivates people to lead?

We will explore each of these money puzzles in turn.

Why this myth matters

The need for money

Sometimes, leaders lead and need no money. William Rodriguez is reputed to have been the last person out of the World Trade Centre on 9/11. The reason he was last out was that he had gone back in to lead people out to safety. He was truly leading, if the definition of leadership is 'taking people where they would not have got by themselves'. His leadership required bravery, not money.

But, for the most part, leaders discover that you cannot change the world without money. Even leaders who eschew wealth or attack capitalism need funding to succeed.

• Mahatma Gandhi famously lived in poverty. His close friend and poet Sarojini Naidu complained to him: 'Do you know how much it costs us to keep you in poverty? A fortune.' This meant he was dependent on wealthy backers such as Ghanshyam Das Birla to keep his campaign going.[2]

- Karl Marx depended on rich capitalist Friedrich Engels to keep him afloat while he wrote *Das Kapital*, paving the way for the communist revolution.[3] He needed capitalists to destroy capitalism.
- Most of the great explorers who go through huge hardship on their adventures spend little of their lives actually exploring. More prosaically, they spend most of their lives raising money from investors, speeches and books. Living in extreme hardship can be extremely expensive.

Money is the rocket fuel of ambition. A great idea without any funding is a pipe dream. To turn ideas into reality, leaders need money. This is true whether you are leading a nation or a service team. In practice, money is one of the three pillars of successful leadership:

- Idea: You need an idea about how you will make a difference.
- People: You need a great team to turn dreams into reality.
- Money: This is the fuel for your idea and your people.

The importance of money is reflected in who becomes CEO. Of the top 100 publicly quoted firms in the UK, over half the CEOs have a financial background and a quarter are qualified chartered accountants.[4] A quarter of Fortune 500 firm CEOs were appointed from a CFO role.[5] The finance function is taking control. And money does not matter for leadership?

Leaders and wealth

Pay of the median S&P 500 CEO is now 203 times that of the median employee.[6] In 1965, the CEO earned just 15 times the compensation of the median employee. There has been an explosion of pay at the top. Average CEO compensation at top firms now runs at $15.5 million annually.[7] Various reasons for high pay are put forward:

- *It's tough at the top*. We have already seen (Myth 30) that it is tougher in the middle than at the top.
- *CEOs have little job security*. Median CEO tenure at S&P 500 firms is now 6.6 years, up one year since 2005.[8] Job security is rising and is better than that of staff, who have median job tenure of 4.2 years. Only 16 per cent of CEOs who move on are dismissed.[9]
- *If we don't pay top dollar we will lose top talent*. There is no evidence of top CEOs moving from one firm to another for a salary increase.
- *The CEO makes all the difference*. Pay certainly seems to make a difference, in the wrong direction. Research shows that of 1,500 large firms, higher executive compensation led to worse performance over three years.[10] Despite performance-linked pay, there is no evidence that pay drives better performance.
- *It is the market rate*. But the market fails on top pay: every board thinks they want an above-average CEO so they pay above average, which means the average rises remorselessly. The problem will get far worse before it gets better.

One question this raises is whether money is required to motivate people to become leaders. There is no reason for this to be the case. People normally want to lead to make a difference, whether it is in a community group or elsewhere. Making a difference and making money are different concepts. Great wealth is not a sign of great leadership, nor should it be required to motivate people to lead.

Another view is that perhaps we should not worry about high CEO pay. We do not complain about the huge sums earned by football stars, film stars and entrepreneurs.

In the UK, the average pay of footballers in the top division has risen even faster than that of CEOs. In 2000 they were earning an average of £10,000 per week;[11] by 2021 it had risen to £60,000 per week.[12] This includes many journeyman players; top players earn over to £20 million a year in salary, excluding endorsements and other commercial activity.

The public find it easier to accept high pay for film and sports stars because the contract between us and the star is very transparent. We volunteer to pay the star and we watch him or her perform; we see what they do and we can stop paying when we no longer like what they do. A different sort of transparency works for entrepreneurs. We can all see that they started and built something themselves and they deserve the rewards for that.

There is no such transparency for CEO pay. We see that they earn a lot, but it is not clear what they deliver in return, nor can we give clear 'consent' to their pay, unlike film and sports stars.

So what is the problem with high CEO pay?

- Breakdown in trust and respect for the leaders within the business. When the CEO demands that staff show passion and loyalty, and then downsizes and fires 20 per cent of the staff while pocketing millions more in compensation, a serious trust problem arises. It looks like the CEO is acting in pure self-interest.

- Excess pay leads to social conflict. Popular movements are on the rise in the democratic world, to the consternation of the elite. But this is not surprising. Real hourly salaries for production and non-supervisory roles in America peaked in 1973 at $23.24; that peak was not reached again until 2019.[13] At the same time, business leaders were enriching themselves to an unprecedented degree.

- Public loss of trust in business and its leadership. The 2021 Ipsos MORI veracity index shows that business leaders are one of the least trusted professions that exist: only 31 per cent of the population trust leaders to tell the truth.[14] At least that is better than government ministers, who are only trusted by 19 per cent of the population. If leaders are seen to be greedy liars then a popular backlash against the elite is not far behind.

- CEOs start to believe that they are special. If you are paid very highly and treated very well, that is evidence that you must be special. This creates a circular logic: 'I am special so I deserve top rewards, which shows I am special.'

Lessons for leaders

There are four possible lessons for leaders:

1 If you want to change the world, money is the fuel you need for your idea and for your team.
2 Become money literate – know how to raise money, allocate resources and budget well.

3 Know your own motivation. What do you really want in life, and how much money do you need to achieve it? Do you really need to earn over $15 million a year, and what would you do with it anyway? Self-worth is more than net worth.

4 If you want to lead people where they would not have got by themselves, it helps if they trust and respect you. Excess pay erodes trust.

Boards or shareholders need to get a grip, otherwise government will get a grip, and it is unlikely to be a warm embrace.

Conclusion

Money matters in leadership. It matters because it is hard to make a difference without money, and it matters because leaders (or at least CEOs) now earn unprecedented amounts of money, which helps to fuel popular discontent with elites. While rarely spoken about, this is not a myth.

Notes

1 If you want to find out why the dog did not bark, read the short story 'Silver Blaze' by Sir Arthur Conan Doyle in *The Memoirs of Sherlock Holmes* (1892).

2 S Rushdie. Mahatma Gandhi, *Time*, 2007, http://content.time.com/time/world/article/0,8599,1653029,00.html (archived at https://perma.cc/6JAK-K4RJ)

3 Engels' wealth was largely inherited: he was the eldest son of a wealthy textile manufacturer.

4   Association of Corporate Treasurers, More than half of FTSE 100 CEOs have a background in finance, nd, www.treasurers.org/hub/treasurer-magazine/more-half-ftse-100-ceos-have-background-finance (archived at https://perma.cc/4535-T4ZA)

5   R Crump. Quarter of FTSE 100 bosses are qualified accountants, The CFO, 2015, https://the-cfo.io/2015/05/19/quarter-of-ftse-100-bosses-are-qualified-accountants/ (archived at https://perma.cc/5P8V-SXJD)

6   L Mishel and J Kandra. CEO pay has skyrocketed 1,322% since 1978: CEOs were paid 351 times as much as a typical worker in 2020, Economic Policy Institute, 2021, www.epi.org/publication/ceo-pay-in-2020 (archived at https://perma.cc/8EYS-LJCK)

7   New York City Central Labor Council. Average S&P 500 company CEO-to-worker pay ratio rises to 299–1, 2021, www.nycclc.org/news/2021-07/average-sp-500-company-ceo-worker-pay-ratio-rises-299-1 (archived at https://perma.cc/6M58-L99F)

8   M Tonello and J Schloetzer. CEO succession practices in the Russell 3000 and S&P 500, Harvard Law School Forum on Corporate Governance, 2021, https://corpgov.law.harvard.edu/2021/01/15/ceo-succession-practices-in-the-russell-3000-and-sp-500 (archived at https://perma.cc/9D2Q-MFAB)

9   J Karaian. Rise of the number crunchers: How CFOs took over the boardroom, Quartz, 2014, http://qz.com/179301/how-cfos-took-over-the-boardroom/ (archived at https://perma.cc/8DYU-ADRW)

10 L Mishel and A Davis. Top CEOs make 300 times more than typical workers, Economic Policy Institute, 2015, www.epi.org/publication/top-ceos-make-300-times-more-than-workers-pay-growth-surpasses-market-gains-and-the-rest-of-the-0-1-percent/ (archived at https://perma.cc/X2BM-MT3B)

11 M Tonello. New statistics and cases of CEO succession in the S&P 500, Harvard Law School, 2015 https://corpgov.law.harvard.edu/2015/04/23/new-statistics-and-cases-of-ceo-succession-in-the-sp-500/ (archived at https://perma.cc/E8VX-VLW9); M Cooper, H Gulen and P Raghavendra Rau. Performance for pay? The relation between CEO incentive compensation and future stock price performance, SSRN, 2010, https://papers.ssrn.com/sol3/papers.cfm?abstract_id=1572085 (archived at https://perma.cc/7QW8-BWKY)

12   PFSA. Football wages: How much do footballers gets paid? 2022, https://thepfsa.co.uk/football-wages-how-much-do-footballers-get-paid (archived at https://perma.cc/VS7L-Z82H)

13   World Economic Forum. 50 years of US wages, in one chart, 2019, www.weforum.org/agenda/2019/04/50-years-of-us-wages-in-one-chart/ (archived at https://perma.cc/X6BJ-U9HU)

14   Ipsos MORI. *Ipsos MORI Veracity Index 2021: Trust in professions survey*, 2021, www.ipsos.com/sites/default/files/ct/news/documents/2021-12/trust-in-professions-veracity-index-2021-ipsos-mori_0.pdf (archived at https://perma.cc/WM2Q-K6WS)

MYTH 35

Leaders are popular role models

Leaders tend to underestimate the influence they have.

Try this simple exercise. Think of some of the bosses you have worked for. Remember what they achieved. Now try to remember what they were like. What do you remember the most?

The chances are that you remembered little, if anything, about what they really achieved or what difference they made. But you will probably remember vividly what they were like: the sort of clothes they wore, what they looked like, how they talked, what sort of character they were, whether you liked them, and whether they were popular as a leader.

Now think about how you will be remembered: will you be remembered for what you achieve or for what you are like? And how do you want to be remembered? Do you want people to like you?

In practice, all leaders are remembered mainly as role models. Some role models are good and others are bad. Some leaders are popular and others less so. Whether being a good role model is tied up with also being popular is something this myth will explore.

Why this myth matters

The idea of a role model is usually a positive one. A role model is someone we would like to emulate, and a leader should be held up as an aspirational role model. Why would we want to work for someone we despise or dislike?

But leaders can mistake being an aspirational role model for popularity. This can be a recipe for weakness in a business setting. Good ways to gain popularity include:

- not giving people bad news
- not stretching people and demanding that they achieve more
- accepting second best and not complaining
- always adjusting your diary to suit the needs of others
- keeping a bowl of candy on your desk for passers-by (and yourself)

The popularity problem is acute for leaders in democracies. We expect them to be positive role models, but elections are essentially auctions where different sorts of promises are made to different parts of the electorate. The side which bids the most to the most people wins, but then suffers winner's curse: they have to make good on impossible promises. If politicians were truly honest role models, they would not make promises and they would not get elected. If they want to get elected, they have to make promises they cannot keep. Then no one trusts them. Part of the fault is with the politicians; part of the problem is with us in voting for the impossible.

Leaders can be positive or negative role models; either way, they set the tone for their team. Machiavelli assumed that a leader cannot be both loved and feared, so he chose fear as the true currency of leadership. There are still a few bosses who operate like that. They are the psychopaths who believe that a team player is someone who does what they are told. But love and fear is a false choice. There is a stronger currency of leadership than fear or love. The true currency of leadership is respect and trust. Being both respected and trusted has a lot more to do with being a positive role model than popularity.

Leaders tend to underestimate the influence they have in terms of substance, style and learning.

Substance

In terms of substance, leaders have to use words carefully. What you say will be used and misused to justify actions far away from you. One senior leader was shocked to find that the office was being redesigned on the basis that that was what he wanted. The leader had no view and had not expressed an opinion, but it had proven an expedient way for a manager to force through the redesign. If managers want something done, the easy way to push it is to claim that is what the boss wants: no one argues with the boss.

Style

At least with matters of substance, you can see what is happening and you can deal with it. Matters of style are much harder to deal with, and the consequences can be much more damaging. If you find that you have a team which is Machiavellian, low on trust, competitive and individualistic you can blame the team, or you can look in the mirror. Teams pick up their behaviours from their leader, for better or for worse. This means you have to pay constant attention not just to what you do, but to how you do it.

Learning

We saw in Myth 28 that emerging leaders learn heavily from their boss, both good and bad lessons. You are constantly under the microscope, with your team peering at your every action. This is where you are a highly influential role model.

Lessons for leaders

Effective leadership is not something that just happens. You cannot just turn up in the morning and start leading. To lead well requires conscious effort. It is obvious that you need to make conscious effort and conscious decisions around matters of substance. But since you will be remembered more for how you are than for what you do, you also have to make conscious decisions about how you behave. Your decisions will influence how your team reacts and performs.

Manage your mood

If you come into the office feeling gloomy, your gloom will soon spread like a major depression across the office. Your team will try to avoid seeing you, knowing that any discussion will be less than productive, and their avoidance will probably just annoy you even more. Leaders have to learn the basic truth that we can choose how we feel. We are accountable for our feelings. If we want to feel gloomy and suspicious, that is our choice. If we want to be positive and professional, that is also our choice. As humans, we have good days and bad days. On good days, it is easy to project the right mood. The real test comes on bad days. That is when leaders have to make a conscious choice about how they want to present themselves to the team. Choose well.

Manage your style

You are who you are and there is no point in trying to become someone else. The challenge for the leader is to become the best of who you are. If you are deeply analytical and not great with people, then that is how you are. Recognize this and, in your deeply analytical way, work out what you need to do to bring people along with you: use your strength to address your weakness.

As a role model, make conscious decisions about how you want to be seen. You will not get any direct feedback on this, but you will get clear indirect feedback in the way that your team behaves: they will be following or reacting to your lead. They will remember you for how you are. How do you want to be remembered?

Encourage learning

Since everyone is watching you and learning from you, make this process explicit, not implicit. This does not require you to ask people for feedback, because no one gives honest feedback to their boss face to face. But you can instil the basic discipline of debriefs. The Red Arrows, the UK air display team, do this after every show and every practice because they chase perfection and mistakes can be fatal. In the debrief, the hierarchy is suspended: the focus is purely on the performance and how it can be improved. Asking WWW ('What went well?') and EBI ('Even better if...?') is a positive and non-threatening way of extracting the learning (see Myth 26).

This learning will help your team improve fast, and it will also help you to build trust and respect by showing that you are willing to stretch people, ask that they achieve more and not accept second best. Asking WWW and EBI requires strong-form honesty. Weak-form honesty is politicians' honesty: they assume they are honest until they have been convicted in court of lying. But in day-to-day life, leaders are not presumed innocent until they are proved guilty. Strong-form honesty does not permit shading the truth or omitting vital information. The challenge for the leader is to tell the truth in a way which is positive and constructive, with the hope that your team members will take your lead and do the same.

Respect lasts longer than popularity, and will serve you well in hard times as well as good. It is the way to high performance, not adequate performance. You do not need to be feared or loved: you need to be respected. And once you are respected, you will be remembered as a positive role model.

Conclusion

All leaders are also role models, for better or worse. So this isn't a myth. But this myth is easily misinterpreted as indicating that leaders are only positive role models, when many are less than positive. Many of the actions leaders might take to be popular will not gain them the trust and respect necessary to be a positive role model. The pursuit of popularity can be lethal to the effectiveness of leaders. Instead, leaders have to consider their impact in terms of substance, style and learning. Those who don't can easily have a negative effect on their team.

Index

Other titles in the Myths series

ISBN: 9781398607781   ISBN: 9781398607828   ISBN: 9781398608573

ISBN: 9781398608153   ISBN: 9781398608276   ISBN: 9781398607743